BRIGHT NOTES

HOWARDS END AND A PASSAGE TO INDIA BY E. M. FORSTER

Intelligent Education

INFLUENCE PUBLISHERS

Nashville, Tennessee

BRIGHT NOTES: Howards End and A Passage to India
www.BrightNotes.com

No part of this publication may be used or reproduced in any manner whatsoever without written permission, except in the case of brief quotations in critical articles and reviews. For permissions, contact Influence Publishers http://www.influencepublishers.com.

ISBN: 978-1-645421-04-7 (Paperback)
ISBN: 978-1-645421-05-4 (eBook)

Published in accordance with the U.S. Copyright Office Orphan Works and Mass Digitization report of the register of copyrights, June 2015.

Originally published by Monarch Press.
Sandra M. Gilbert, 1965
2020 Edition published by Influence Publishers.

Interior design by Lapiz Digital Services. Cover Design by Thinkpen Designs.

Printed in the United States of America.

Library of Congress Cataloging-in-Publication Data forthcoming.
Names: Intelligent Education
Title: BRIGHT NOTES: Howards End and A Passage to India
Subject: STU004000 STUDY AIDS / Book Notes

CONTENTS

INTRODUCTION TO E. M. FORSTER

Edward Morgan Forster was born in London in 1879, the son of an architect, who died shortly after the child's birth. As a boy, he lived in Hertfordshire, in the house which was later to become the central symbol of *Howards End*. He attended Tonbridge School, a typical English "Public School," which he disliked intensely, and later, King's College, Cambridge, where he studied classics and history and was quite happy. There he became friendly with the circle of intellectuals which subsequently came to be called the "Bloomsbury Group," because most of them lived near each other in the Bloomsbury section of London.

THE BLOOMSBURY GROUP

The Bloomsbury Group included many of the most important British intellectuals of the early twentieth century: Lytton Strachy, whose Queen Victoria and Eminent Victorians are classics of biography; Roger Fry, a well-known art critic and aesthetic theorist; Virginia Woolf, the novelist, and her husband Leonard, the publisher; Bertrand Russell, the philosopher-mathematician; and Maynard Keynes, the economist. All were influenced by the ideas of the Cambridge philosopher, G. E. Moore, whose major work, Principia Ethica, was published in 1903, shortly after Forster had left the University. Moore believed, in K. W. Gransden's words, that "the contemplation of beauty in art and the cultivation of personal relations were the most important things in life," and we can easily see how these views are reflected in *Howards End* and *A Passage to India.*

Forster himself, however, has often rejected the attempts of literary historians to identify him wholly with the Bloomsbury Group. And indeed, though Bloomsbury has been accused of "exclusiveness" and "remoteness from other ways of life," Forster is often exempted from these attacks, even by the movement's bitterest critics.

EARLY WRITING

After leaving Cambridge, E. M. Forster began to write short stories and novels. In fact, his three earliest novels appeared in rapid succession while he was still in his twenties-*Where Angels Fear to Tread* (1905), a story partly set in Italy, where Forster lived for a time after graduation; *The Longest Journey* (1907), set in Cambridge; and *A Room With a View* (1908), again partly set in Italy. Finally, in 1910, this series of novels was climaxed by *Howards End*, his most mature work to date.

MID-CAREER

After the publication of *Howards End*, Forster stopped writing novels for fourteen years. He turned to literary journalism, and in 1912-13 he went to India with G. Lowes Dickinson, a philosophy Don at Cambridge whom he much admired and whose biography he later wrote (*Goldsworthy Lowes Dickinson,*

1936). During World War I he engaged in civilian war work in Alexandria, later producing a travel book about that city (*Alexandria, A History and a Guide*, 1922). After the war he returned to work as a journalist in London.

A PASSAGE TO INDIA

In 1921 Forster went to India as secretary to the Maharajah of Dewas State Senior. This experience, combined with his earlier trip, resulted in 1924 in *A Passage to India*, which he finished in England. The book was generally acclaimed as his finest novel, and it won a number of prizes throughout the world.

ASPECTS OF THE NOVEL

In 1927 Forster delivered a series of lectures at Cambridge, which eventually developed into his most important critical pronouncement, *Aspects of the Novel* (1927). A reading of this work in conjunction with a careful examination of Forster's own major novels will prove most rewarding for a student interested in relating the author's critical theory to his creative practice.

OTHER WORKS

Other works by E. M. Forster include *The Celestial Omnibus* (1923) and *The Eternal Moment* (1928), two collections of short stories; *Abinger Harvest* (1936), a group of essays; and *The Hill of Devi* (1953), a collection of letters and reminiscences about India which are especially fascinating to a critic of *A Passage to India*.

FORSTER TODAY

Forster, who is still fairly active in the literary world, lives at Cambridge, where he has been an Honorary Fellow of King's College since 1946. His country has showered numerous honors upon him, including membership in the Order of Companions of Honor (awarded by Queen Elizabeth II), and he is generally considered one of the major British novelists of this century.

HOWARDS END AND A PASSAGE TO INDIA

These two novels are usually ranked as E. M. Forster's maturest and most brilliant books; indeed, though they are separated by a span of fourteen years in which the author produced little or no creative work, they comprise, together, the final and culminating novels in a series of five books which got increasingly better as the novelist's abilities ripened. Both works, moreover, have many **themes** and ideas in common (see the Sample Essay Questions and Answers), and it is interesting to notice how the years which intervened between them modified Forster's handling of these persisting themes.

Generally speaking, *Howards End* seems more optimistic than *A Passage to India*, and perhaps more sentimental. It focuses in a semi-idealistic way on England, its past, present and future, and in doing so it tends to romanticize the traditions of the past, while clearsightedly prophesying the trends of the future. *A Passage to India*, on the other hand, is obviously the product of a writer who is older, tougher, more pessimistic, and as a result this book seems more condensed, more intense, and less discursive. It gazes steadily and realistically at the past and the present; if it has any hope at all, it is only a minor and vague hope for the future, implied rather than stated.

Nevertheless, it is easy to see that the thinker who advised "Only connect" in *Howards End* was still obsessed with the problems of connection and "separateness" when he came to write *A Passage to India*. Only now, in the later book, had he begun to think connection was no longer a very serious possibility; if it was not actually an impossibility, he certainly thought it an improbability. And perhaps this was because in *Howards End* Forster confined himself pretty strictly to novel-writing as a kind of social science: England in the book was simply England, the nation, the social structure. But in *A Passage to India* Forster fictionalized metaphysics: India stood for more than India; as in Whitman's poem, "Passage to India," from which he drew his title, Forster's India became a kind of cosmic symbol. Thus the hopes and dreams of the young man who wrote *Howards End*-hopes and dreams which could be nourished in the man-centered, social context of the earlier book-had to be abandoned by the wiser, older man who wrote the later book and knew that man's dreams are infinitely small and petty in comparison to the impersonal, indifferent universe in which he finds himself.

To the average reader, *Howards End* and *A Passage to India* may seem to be rather simple and open in their style and structure, but while it is true, of course, that they are easy-indeed, delightful-to read and to understand, they are in fact extraordinarily complex in their use of recurring motifs, themes, symbols and images. This study of the two novels will try to deal with as many of these poetic devices as possible throughout the Detailed Summary, but if an attentive reader studies the texts of the two books carefully, he will find each reading of *Howards End* and *A Passage to India* increasingly rewarding. For E. M. Forster's greatest achievement as a novelist is the intricate structure of ideas and the elaborate texture of images which he is able to maintain, and through which he reflects and refracts his vision of the world, throughout these two novels.

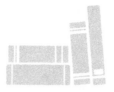

HOWARDS END

CHAPTER ONE

The first chapter of *Howards End* consists of two letters from Helen Schlegel (who we later learn is a girl of twenty-one) to her older sister Meg (twenty-nine). Helen is visiting the Wilcoxes, a family whom the Schlegels have met abroad (in Germany), at their suburban home, Howards End. Helen's letters seem quite routine-descriptions of the house, family activities, members of the party, etc. - until in the last one-line note she drops a bombshell: "Dearest, dearest Meg, -I do not know what you will say: Paul and I are in love-the younger son who only came here on Wednesday."

Comment

Though Helen's descriptive, chatty letters may not seem to open the book with any very obvious drama, they are actually one of the best possible ways of introducing the reader to some of the novel's principal characters and themes. First of all, of course, there is Helen, whose rather mercurial, enthusiastic personality is quickly revealed in her letters. Furthermore, the more conventional "bourgeois" nature of the Wilcoxes is shown through Helen's memories of Mr. Wilcox's "bullying porters," and through her story of his scolding her for advocating women's rights. We see that for some reason Helen, the sensitive intellectual type, is strangely attracted to these rather "nouveau-riche," cricket-playing Wilcoxes, and we guess that the relationship between Schlegels and Wilcoxes is going to form an important part of the plot of *Howards End*.

We are also introduced to Mrs. Wilcox, so oddly different from her husband and children as she trails lovingly across the lawn in her beautiful dress, and the **theme** of hay fever which makes its appearance here for the first time helps to emphasize her differentness. All the Wilcoxes have hay fever which forces them indoors out of the lovely garden except Mrs. Wilcox, who goes about with her hands full of hay, sniffing it and never sneezing. The house was hers to begin with, we eventually learn, and her lack of hay fever is thus almost a mark of grace, a sign that she belongs, whereas the others don't.

Finally, when Helen writes her third note, about being in love with Paul, the youngest son, the urgency of her message sets it off from the casual chatty **exposition** for which her letters were first used and plunges the reader directly into one of the dramatic crises of the book.

CHAPTER TWO

In this chapter we are introduced to the other important Schlegel, Helen's sister Margaret, who is shown at the breakfast table with her Aunt Juley (Mrs. Munt), a kindly, old-fashioned, very British busybody who has come to keep Margaret company while Helen is away. Margaret has just received Helen's note about Paul, and she is quite naturally upset. She explains to Aunt Juley that she knows rather little about the Wilcoxes, that she and Helen had met them on a tour in Germany, and that both sisters had been invited down to Howards End for the week, but the illness (from hayfever) of the third Schlegel-Tibby, the girls' fifteen-year-old brother-had prevented Margaret from accompanying Helen.

Aunt Juley offers to go down at once to Howards End to investigate the matter, but Margaret, feeling strongly that her aunt (who calls the sisters "odd girls") can never understand Helen, refuses to let her. "I must go myself," she insists. Aunt Juley replies frankly that Margaret is sure to botch the situation. "... You would offend the whole of these Wilcoxes by asking one of your impetuous questions - not" (she adds) "that one minds offending them" Margaret, however, remains determined. Mrs. Munt very practically feels that the engagement, if engagement there is, must be broken off at once. But Margaret, who has rather more faith in her sister, plans to proceed more slowly.

It soon develops, though, that Tibby's ridiculous hay fever is worse than ever; a doctor is sent for, pronounces him quite bad, and Margaret is finally forced to accept Aunt Juley's offer and dispatch her to Howards End with a note for Helen. She warns her, however, "not to be drawn into discussing the engagement. Give my letter to Helen, and say whatever you feel yourself, but do keep clear of the relatives." Margaret doesn't approve of scenes - and certainly not of "uncivilized" wrangling over marriages.

Mrs. Munt duly departs from King's Cross Station after promising to carry out her niece's instructions. But when

Margaret returns home after seeing her aunt to the train, she is met by another message from her sister-a telegram this time, stating "All over. Wish I had never written. Tell no one. Helen" . . . "But Aunt Juley was gone-gone irrevocably, and no power on earth could stop her."

Comment

This chapter continues the delineation of the Schlegel family, begun in Chapter One with Helen's letters. We see Margaret, the rather less flighty but still "impulsive" older sister, running her solid, well-established household at Wickham Place in London with competence and compassion. She is "not beautiful, not supremely brilliant, but filled with . . . a profound vivacity, a continual and sincere response to all that she encountered in her path through life." The Wickham Place house itself, located in a quiet, rather aristocratic "backwater" of London, symbolizes the family's established dignity and culture. Mrs. Munt, the sister of Helen's, Margaret's and Tibby's British mother, represents the English side of their background, and a brief discussion between her and Margaret of the relative merits of the English and the Germans (the Schlegels are German on their father's side) introduces the **theme** of Englishness, which is to become more important later on. Tibby's hay fever, on the other hand, expands a **theme** already introduced-the **theme** of hay fever as a kind of symbolic allergy to the natural world-which is so significant a part of the lives of certain characters in this novel.

CHAPTER THREE

"Most complacently" Aunt Juley proceeds on her irrevocable way to Howards End. She is glad to be of service to her nieces, especially since their independent personalities usually lead them to keep her at arm's length. Even when they were left motherless as children (their mother had died giving birth to Tibby, fifteen years before the opening of the book, when Helen was five and Margaret thirteen) their father had refused all Mrs. Munt's offers of help, with Margaret's concurrence, and when their father too had died, five years later, Margaret had again refused Aunt Juley's offer to keep house for them. Conservative, well-meaning and incurably curious, Mrs. Munt has for years tried to mind her own business, but she has a powerful itch to interfere, if only by advising the girls on what stocks to buy ("Home Rails" rather than "Foreign Things").

After an hour's journey northward Aunt Juley arrives at Wilton, near Howards End, where she accidentally meets a young man who she is told is "the younger Mr. Wilcox." Thinking he is Paul, Helen's new fiancé, she gratefully accepts his offer to run her up to the house in the family motor, which he has just taken out "for a spin" and to do some errands. He seems surprisingly cool at the mention of Helen, but Mrs. Munt, who tends to be rather unobservant, doesn't notice this, and within a few minutes she has disobeyed Margaret's instructions and confronted the young man with the entire story of his (Paul's) supposed relationship with Helen. Of course, it comes out almost immediately-to the accompaniment of much embarrassment-that this younger Mr. Wilcox is not Paul but Charles, Paul's older brother, who becomes violently angry at the news of his brother's engagement. Paul "has to make his way out in Nigeria," he storms, conducting the family rubber business, and "couldn't think of marrying for years," especially not a girl like Helen, who is definitely the wrong type in Charles' very emphatic opinion. Mrs. Munt, of course, grows furious in her turn, exclaiming that if she were a man she would "box his ears . . . for that last remark," and, as Forster puts it, they play the game of "Capping Families" all the way to the house.

When they arrive at Howards End, Charles is on the verge of precipitating a showdown with Paul when Mrs. Wilcox makes her first, very memorable appearance, "trailing noiselessly over the lawn" with a wisp of hay in her hands. In her gentle, unaffected way she sees that there is trouble, and going straight to the heart of things-without any social pretenses-she explains that the engagement has been broken off and sends the embattled Schlegels and Wilcoxes off in different directions to recover their tempers before lunch.

Comment

In this chapter the picture of Aunt Juley is filled in further, as is that of the Wilcoxes. Strait-laced as she seems, there is "a vein of coarseness" in Mrs. Munt, which Margaret may have recognized in her desire to avoid sending her aunt on this mission in the first place. Similarly, there is a vein of coarseness, indeed a river of apoplectic bad temper, in the Wilcoxes, especially Charles, which was first hinted at in Helen's phrase about Mr. Wilcox's "bullying porters" and which is to prove most important in the **denouement** (solution) of the plot.

Most important in this chapter, however, is our first real introduction to Mrs. Wilcox. She is just as graceful and magical as she seemed in Helen's letters, only more profoundly so. A gentle woman of about fifty, she seems part of the small, beautifully proportioned house at Howards End, a kind of genius loci or spirit of the place, and, as Forster puts it, "one knew that she worshipped the past, and that the instinctive wisdom the past can alone bestow had descended upon her-that wisdom to which we give the clumsy name of aristocracy." This whole question of the past-of tradition and the individual's share in it-is to become one of the novel's most important themes, a theme whose embodiment throughout most of the book will be the enigmatically beautiful and serene Mrs. Wilcox.

CHAPTER FOUR

Helen and Aunt Juley return to London "in a state of collapse," but Mrs. Munt soon recovers, self-righteously congratulating herself on having spared "poor Margaret" such a dreadful experience. Helen, however, is more seriously upset; she seems, indeed, to have fallen in love, "not with an individual, but with a family."

Helen-indeed all the Schlegels-is an intellectual and a liberal, with all the standard enlightened views on social reform, women's suffrage, art, literature, etc. The Wilcoxes, on the other hand, are a robust, athletic family of businessmen. They think all the Schlegels' pet ideas and projects are nonsense. Except for Mrs. Wilcox, they are rude to servants, arrogant to underlings and utterly insensitive to culture. Helen, who has never encountered such people before, who has always lived a sheltered life in the best intellectual circles of London, can't help being fascinated by the Wilcoxes, who strike her like a breath of fresh air. Her affair with Paul - no more passed between them than a brief kiss, really (which, however, meant a good deal in 1910, the date of the novel)-was the result.

In their conversations after the event, Helen and Margaret - they are compulsive talkers - try hard to understand the difference between the Schlegel and Wilcox ways of life, and to decide which is preferable. They finally decide that the Wilcoxes live an outer life of "telegrams and anger," a life which fails to withstand moments of crisis as their own inner life of personal relationships and commitment can. Gradually they forget the

Wilcoxes' momentary magnetism and revert to the style of living for which their English-German background has prepared them. Their father, Forster tells us, was an idealistic German, of the Hegel-Kant variety, who left his native land when it became too commercial and imperialistic for him. "It was his hope that the clouds of materialism obscuring the Fatherland would part in time, and the mild, intellectual light re-emerge." How are the offspring of such a dreamer to reconcile themselves to an England in which the same imperialism, hastened by Wilcoxes, has begun to predominate? Trying hard to do the right thing, the two girls go to meetings and rule a kind of blue-stocking salon at Wickham Place. Of the two, Helen is more popular, Margaret more sensible. As for their brother Tibby, he is not of much importance as yet - "an intelligent man of sixteen, but dyspeptic and difficile."

Comment

This chapter gives further information about the Schlegels' background and their reaction to the Wilcoxes. It also provides a breathing space in which the pace of the plot can be relaxed for a moment before the introduction of important new characters in Chapter Five.

CHAPTER FIVE

Here we are introduced to a character who represents the third important social grouping in the book, for if the Schlegels represent the solidly established intellectuals in the middle of the middle-class financial scale, and the Wilcoxes the newly rich industrialists at the top of the scale, Leonard Bast, the poor young clerk who meets Helen and Margaret at a concert, stands for the struggling, impoverished white-collar worker at the bottom of the scale.

The chapter opens with a discussion of Beethoven's Fifth Symphony - "the most sublime noise that has ever penetrated into the ear of man." The cultivated Schlegels, Tibby, Margaret and Helen, along with their Aunt Juley, a German cousin, Frieda Mosebach, and her "young man," Herr Liesecke, are attending a performance of the symphony. Mrs. Munt and Helen notice that Margaret, at the end of the row, is talking to a strange young man. Mrs. Munt is curious about him, but Helen's mind wanders, as she listens to the music, to thoughts of a goblin walking through the universe, whose footfalls seem to be suggested by the rhythm of the drums. "Panic and emptiness! Panic and emptiness!" she thinks, is what Beethoven sees at the heart of things. And she too, she reflects, has had a glimpse of panic and emptiness-at the heart of the Wilcoxes' world, in the recent debacle with Paul. Much moved, she rushes out of the concert hall after the symphony is over, without waiting for the next number.

But Helen, in her haste to be gone, has inadvertently taken an umbrella belonging to Leonard Bast, the strange young man with whom Margaret has struck up a conversation. Leonard suspects, as incredible as it seems, that Helen has stolen it, and that the whole Schlegel family party may be nothing but a ring of thieves. His suspicion, quite obvious from his voice and face though he makes no open accusations, sickens Margaret so that she cannot attend to the Brahms, which follows, at all. As soon as the concert is over, she invites the young clerk to walk her home so that he can get his umbrella. He accepts, and after some awkward conversation they arrive at Wickham Place, where Helen returns the umbrella, after inadvertently commenting on how "appalling" its condition is. Though Margaret wants to ask the poor young man to tea, he flushes with embarrassment and shame at Helen's casual cruelty, and rushes away into the city, leaving neither name nor card behind. Margaret and Helen are miserable too, but Mrs. Munt, ever practical, remarks that after all he might have been a thief and it's just as well not to invite a stranger to tea so precipitously. Then the well-fed Tibby, indifferent to the general pathos of things, brews some expensive tea and the plight of the "ill-fed boy" is, at least for the moment, forgotten.

Comment

This chapter has an almost self-contained structure, like a short story or a little essay on the difference between the rich and the poor, the well - and the ill-fed. Helen, casual and, as Margaret puts it, "ramshackly," couldn't care less about a material object like an umbrella; she has more material things than she knows what to do with. But in the mind of the struggling Leonard Bast, there can be only one reason for making off with another person's umbrella-because one needs it, or the money one can get for it. His suspicion, his nervousness, his social awkwardness and embarrassment are all strikingly set off against the wealthy and civilized ease of the Schlegels. And at the end, Aunt Juley's rather natural suspicion of him-after all, the Schlegel plate is a good deal more tempting than a Bast umbrella-provides the final touch of irony.

CHAPTER SIX

Now we follow Leonard Bast home to his dingy basement flat on the other side of London. Though he is not "very poor," he hovers dangerously near the brink of poverty, and so close to the bottom of the lower middle-class that he could easily slip, with one false step, into the unthinkable abyss of the lower-class. He is a white-collar worker, a half-educated clerk leading a grubby subterranean life in the great city, with aspirations toward culture and style that he has not the means to fulfill.

When he gets home, Leonard makes himself some weak tea and settles down to read Ruskin. He is trying to learn prose style from that wealthy master of art appreciation, and Forster emphasizes the **irony** of "the rich man in his gondola" describing Venice for the benefit of poor, hopeless Leonard Bast: "The voice in the gondola rolled on, piping melodiously of Effort and Self-Sacrifice, full of high purpose, full of beauty, full even of sympathy and the love of men, yet somehow eluding all that was actual and insistent in Leonard's life. For it was the voice of one who had never been dirty or hungry, and had not guessed successfully what dirt and hunger are."

After a while Leonard's mistress, Jacky, comes in. She is a rather faded, cheaply and elaborately attired woman of thirty-three, quite "past her prime" and not at all "respectable." Her appearance underlines Leonard's pathos, for she has somehow inveigled the boy into promising to marry her in a year, when he reaches the age of twenty-one. Yet, we see, there is a certain warmth in their relationship, and the young man prepares an unappetizing supper of packaged soup, canned meat and jello for the two of them with some solicitude. Later, after Jacky has gone to bed, the clerk goes back to reading Ruskin; when Jacky calls him from the bedroom he pretends not to hear her, lost in his futile dream of the rich man's civilization.

Comment

This is probably one of the most affecting chapters in the book, a chapter in which we are made to see on what foundation the ease and style of the Schlegels (and Ruskins) rest, and what laboring classes struggle to support the comfort of the Wilcoxes. Leonard's premature and pathetic relationship with the overblown, over-decorated Jacky will be shown in later chapters to fit even more shockingly into this inequitable social scheme of things.

CHAPTER SEVEN

The morning after the concert Aunt Juley learns that the Wilcoxes have taken a flat in the "ornate block" opposite the Schlegels' unassumingly elegant Wickham Place house. Aunt Juley is very upset over this, fearing, naturally, a recurrence of the Helen-Paul affair. Helen, however, assures her that she no longer has any interest in Wilcoxes, and no matter how often she is cross-examined on the subjects he seems to be genuinely telling the truth.

In a discussion of the whole business with Aunt Juley, Margaret, who is more worried than she wants to admit, remarks that money is what saved the situation with Helen and Paul. If "motor cars and railways" could not have been invoked to separate the lovers, what would have happened? Still, the presence of the Wilcoxes across the street remains irksome; Margaret occasionally sees Evie, the eighteen-year-old daughter of the family, "stating rudely" at her, and she is glad when Helen decides to go to Germany for a vacation with her cousin Frieda Mosebach.

Comment

The contrast with the preceding chapter, in which Leonard and Jacky are shown together, is obvious. Leonard is trapped in an unsuitable relationship by his lack of money; Helen, as Margaret points out, has been freed from what might have been such a trap by her wealth. Even now she has the means to escape an unpleasant situation by leaving the country. Another important contrast-between the unostentatious home in which the Schlegels have lived for thirty years and the Wilcoxes' showy apartment-is also developed in this chapter. The **theme** of houses, of course, was introduced earlier, with the description of Howards End, and this **theme** will become even more important as the book progresses.

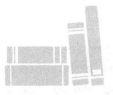

HOWARDS END

CHAPTER EIGHT

This chapter is concerned with the relationship between Margaret Schlegel and Mrs. Wilcox, a strange friendship which is to be one of the pivotal relationships of the book. Forster speculates that it may have been mainly Margaret to whom Mrs. Wilcox was attracted all along, and primarily Margaret whom she had wanted at Howards End that fateful week of the Helen-Paul fiasco. At any rate, two weeks after the Wilcoxes have moved to London Mrs. Wilcox comes to call on Margaret at Wickham Place. Helen is about to leave for Germany, but hasn't yet left, and Margaret is upset at the idea that the dangerous connection with the Wilcoxes may be resumed. She impulsively writes what she herself realizes is a rude note to Mrs. Wilcox, suggesting that their friendship should not be resumed. Mrs. Wilcox, genuinely offended, sends a curt reply: "Dear Miss Schlegel, You should not have written me such a letter. I called to tell you that Paul has gone abroad. Ruth Wilcox."

Burning with embarrassment at her own discourtesy, Margaret rushes across the street to apologize. She finds Mrs. Wilcox in bed, resting and writing letters, and after some explanations on both sides the two are reconciled. They have a strangely affecting (to Margaret), far-ranging conversation. Though they seem to be chatting idly-about Helen's trip to Germany, Charles' engagement and forthcoming marriage to Dolly Fussell, the pretty, shallow daughter of one of Mr. Wilcox's friends, and the young couple's proposed trip to Italy-they are really getting to know and understand each other's inner natures. When the conversation turns to Howards End, especially, Margaret senses in Mrs. Wilcox's nostalgic devotion to the place-to the grand old wych-elm that shades the house and the old pony paddock - an "indescribable" note, perhaps that note of "aristocracy" again which is to give Mrs. Wilcox's character such force throughout the book.

Comment

At this point in the story the contrast between Margaret and Mrs. Wilcox seems rather marked. Mrs. Wilcox seems to be a rural, reticent type, a woman totally immersed in her home and family and utterly uninterested in the outside world, while Margaret, just the opposite, is an active, intellectual Londoner. But the "aristocratic" tradition of England, the serene and orderly past which is embodied in the house at Howards End, will soon bring the two women closer than they can now guess, and a hint of that coming closeness is present in their unexpectedly friendly and warm conversation in this chapter.

CHAPTER NINE

A few days after their first London meeting, Margaret gives a little luncheon party in Mrs. Wilcox's honor. Mrs. Wilcox had told Margaret that she thinks her "inexperienced," but Margaret, who at twenty-nine has practically raised her sister Helen and is still engaged in "bringing up" sixteen-year-old Tibby, believes that "if experience is attainable, she had attained it."

Nevertheless, her luncheon is a dismal failure. Mrs. Wilcox's magic, which Margaret herself feels so strongly, never communicates itself to Margaret's smart London friends - and the brilliance of those smart friends is lost on Mrs. Wilcox. In the midst of intellectual chat about "Thought" and "Art" Mrs. Wilcox sits quietly by, unresponsive and somehow "out of focus" with daily life. All she wants to talk about is her family and Howards End. Yet when she leaves, Margaret feels that she - and not Mrs. Wilcox - is the one who has failed at lunch, that she and her friends are just "gibbering" while Mrs. Wilcox is party to some serene truth that has utterly eluded them. Mrs. Wilcox apologizes for being dull and explains that she hasn't been feeling well; Margaret's friends decide the newcomer is "uninteresting" but Margaret herself is left shaken and uncertain.

Comment

Again the contrast between the two worlds of London and Howards End is emphasized, and again Howards End-through Mrs. Wilcox-seems to be exerting some powerful, inexplicable influence, to be casting some spell which makes the daily dazzlements of the city, its "Thought and Art," strangely dismal.

CHAPTER TEN

Several days pass without any further development of the friendship between Margaret and Mrs. Wilcox, but finally the older woman asks Miss Schlegel-who has become somewhat anxious about their relationship-if she would like to go Christmas shopping with her. Margaret accepts the invitation with alacrity, and the rather oddly assorted pair tour the London department stores together, with Margaret a bit officiously advising Mrs. Wilcox on what presents to get for whom. Mrs. Wilcox seems grateful for her help, yet though she admires Margaret's choice of a Christmas card for her, she rather offhandedly puts off ordering it so that she can "get Evie's opinion" too. Mrs. Wilcoxs vagueness continually defeats Margaret, here as elsewhere, which makes her extraordinary vehemence all the more surprising when Margaret casually mentions that the Schlegels' thirty-year lease is up on Wickham Place and they must soon be househunting. "It is monstrous, Miss Schlegel," she exclaims. "It isn't right. I had no idea that this was hanging over you. I do pity you from the bottom of my heart. To be parted from your house, your father's house-it oughtn't to be allowed. It is worse than dying."

Apparently overtired and near tears at the thought of such an uprooting, Mrs. Wilcox invites Margaret down to Howards End that very afternoon, but Margaret courteously asks that the trip be postponed till more preparations can be made. She hasn't taken Mrs. Wilcox's depth of feeling for the place into enough consideration, however, and is much chagrined when the older woman seems hurt and insulted. Later in the day, after lunch, she resolves to go after all, and crosses the street to Mrs. Wilcox's flat to see if her friend will renew the invitation. But Mrs. Wilcox has already left on her own. Margaret hurries to King's Cross Station, hoping to catch up with her, and when they meet at the ticket booth Mrs. Wilcox greets her with a "grave and happy voice." It seems as though some revelation is at hand-a revelation, perhaps, of the nature of Howards End and the power it exerts over Mrs. Wilcox-when suddenly Mr. Wilcox and Evie appear on the platform. By the sheerest coincidence their vacation in Yorkshire had been interrupted by a "motor smash," and they have been forced to return home by train on this particular afternoon. Of course, the trip to Howards End must be put off, while Mrs. Wilcox is happily and unexpectedly reunited with her family, and Margaret, disappointed, leaves the station alone, the revelation to which she had looked forward irrevocably postponed.

Comment

In this rather important chapter Margaret realizes for the first time the extent of the power Howards End has over Mrs. Wilcox. The meaning of "roots" and "tradition" is slowly being brought home to her as she recognizes that Mrs. Wilcox's vagueness about London life-about such practical matters as Christmas shopping and department stores, etc. - is balanced by a real and concrete fierceness about houses, houses, that is, as homes, symbols of family and tradition which link the individual to his own ancestral past. In this connection, Margaret's indifference and Mrs. Wilcox's intense reaction to the prospective loss of the Schlegel home at Wickham Place are most revealing.

CHAPTER ELEVEN

Rather shockingly, without any transition at all, we discover in this chapter (which begins with the bare words "The funeral was over") that Mrs. Wilcox has just died. No scenes of her sickness are shown directly, but we are later given to understand that she had known she was ill for a long time - while she was living in London, in fact - but had concealed the truth from her family so as not to upset them. That practical, hard-headed family of hers, however, is now suffering "acutely." Mr. Wilcox remembers his wife's "even goodness during thirty years," and the house at Howards End, where the family is staying for the funeral, seems impossible empty, even to Charles and Evie, who "avoided the personal in life" but could not help mourning their mother, no matter how phlegmatically.

Charles has married his Dolly in the interval between the London scenes and Mrs. Wilcox's death, and she, too, is down at Howards End, an empty-headed little thing (her name is an appropriate one), hardly knowing what to do with herself in a house of mourning. The day's mail, however, brings a surprise to the Wilcoxes which pulls them at once out of the trance of grief in which they've been moving. It is a brief note from their mother, addressed to Mr. Wilcox from the nursing home in which she'd died, with instructions that it be forwarded after the funeral. "To my husband": it says. "I should like Miss Schlegel (Margaret) to have Howards End."

Thunderstruck, the Wilcoxes sit down to discuss the matter. Charles wants to know if Margaret may not have exerted "undue influence" on Mrs. Wilcox during her sickness. It seems she had visited her at the nursing home and the Wilcoxes are naturally suspicious, besides being, of course, very hurt that Mrs. Wilcox should have left the one meaningful object in her life to a stranger. At last they convince themselves that the appeal is not legally binding, "had been written in illness, and under the spell of a sudden friendship. . . . To them, Howards End was a house: they could not know that to her it had been a spirit, for which she sought a spiritual heir." Relieved, they tear up the note and throw it in the fire, disposing of Miss Schlegel, so they hope, once and for all. Yet the hurt at what seems to have been Mrs. Wilcox's rejection of her nearest relatives persists, and enables them to begin recovering from their grief rather sooner than they had expected.

Comment

The essential problem posed in this chapter is the question of spiritual, rather than material, inheritance. Mrs. Wilcox seeks "a spiritual heir" for Howards End, which is, after all, her spiritual home. And in some uncanny way, she recognizes that Margaret, of all the people she knows, has the most potential for governing this house. The strange affinity between the two women, which grew so slowly in the earlier chapters of the book, has ripened at last, in this chapter, into action. An action, however, with no consequences, for the Wilcoxes, hard-headed materialists, cannot recognize Mrs. Wilcox's spiritual logic. According to their logic, practical and sensible property-owners that they are, Mrs. Wilcox's personal appeal is "not legally binding" and is therefore to be ignored, as they ignore most personal appeals. And after all, Forster asks, "is it credible that the possessions of the spirit can be bequeathed at all?"

CHAPTER TWELVE

The Wilcoxes were a little worried that Margaret might press her claim to Howards End, but they need not have been, for Margaret knows nothing of Mrs. Wilcox's strange request. In this brief transition chapter, Margaret reflects on the Wilcox character-on its secondary virtues of neatness, decision and obedience, and on the attractiveness that the Wilcoxes, even without the more spiritual Mrs. Wilcox, have for her, despite their "outer life of 'telegrams and anger.'" She corresponds on the subject with her sister Helen, who is still in Germany, no longer has any interest in Wilcoxes, and has received a proposal of marriage from a German, which she rejects. We also learn that Tibby is trying out for a scholarship to Oxford and finds the university appealingly picturesque.

Comment

Tibby's coldness and lack of "personal" feeling indicate that intellectuals of the Schlegel variety can be as closed to "the personal" as practical men of the Wilcox type. In the same way, Margaret, an intellectual, and Mrs. Wilcox, not an intellectual, balanced each other in the extent and depth of their human warmth and desire to "connect" with what is meaningful.

CHAPTER THIRTEEN

Two years pass between chapters twelve and thirteen, two years during which the Schlegels continue to lead a life of "cultured but not ignoble ease." At last the lease of Wickham Place is only nine months away from its expiration date, and Margaret becomes panicky about the need to find a new house. In conversations with Helen and Tibby, now in his second year at Oxford, she tries to decide on a new place to live, most likely a flat in town and a house in the country.

She has also begun to nag Tibby about his lack of direction in life. Though he doesn't need money, she believes that he ought to work at some job or other, if only to be usefully "active" like the Wilcoxes, whom she still admires and occasionally sees socially. Tibby, however, emphatically dislikes the Wilcoxes, like his sister Helen, and prefers - so he says - "civilization" of the Oxford variety to "activity" of the empire-building, Wilcox sort.

In the midst of one of these half-practical, half-theoretical discussions between Tibby and Margaret, Helen bursts in with the news that a strange woman, over-dressed and smelling of orris root, has been to call, "looking for her husband," one "Lan" or "Len." It seems he'd disappeared the day before and the woman, for some mysterious reason, believed he could be found at Wickham Place. Helen is most amused by the whole business, but Margaret, perhaps with a premonition of disaster, warns that the bizarre visit may be more serious than it seems. "It means some horrible volcano smoking somewhere, doesn't it?" she inquires.

Comment

The contrast between "activity and "civilization," between Schlegels and Wilcoxes, is again emphasized in this chapter. Each has its virtues, Margaret seems to be saying, and both must maintain a harmonious balance in order for society to remain stable.

The visit of Mrs. "Lanoline," as Helen dubs her, foreshadows, of course, the reintroduction of Leonard Bast (who has been absent for some pages) into the story.

CHAPTER FOURTEEN

Next day Leonard Bast himself, the "Lan" or "Len" whose wife had intruded on the Schlegels so oddly, comes to call, to explain and apologize for her visit. He reminds Margaret, who doesn't remember it, of their first meeting at the concert, and of the mixup about the umbrella. When the sisters question him as to where he actually had been over the weekend, when his absence disturbed his wife so, he finally admits that he had "walked all the Saturday night" - gone out to the country on the underground (subway) and tramped about in the woods till dawn. Though his talk is full of literary pretensions which rather repel the more sophisticated Schlegels, there is also a note of genuineness in it sometimes which very much attracts them. For example: "But was the dawn wonderful?' asked Helen. With unforgettable sincerity he replied: 'No . . . The dawn was only grey, it was nothing to mention.'"

After more conversation along these lines, the Schlegels invite Leonard to call again, but he, flushed with his first social triumph, is fearful of anticlimaxes. Sensibly enough he remarks that "it is better not to risk a second interview" and leaves, thrilled by his brief encounter with the "romance" of the upper classes.

Poor Leonard has married Jacky, his frowsy, almost middle-aged mistress, in the years since the Schlegels last encountered him, and his life is still predictably grimy and dispiriting. The mixup with Jacky, in fact, occurred because he had kept the visiting card, which Margaret so casually gave him, as another token of "romance", arousing Jacky's curiosity by refusing to explain where he'd gotten it. She naturally "was only capable of drawing one conclusion" - that Margaret was a secret amour of Leonard's -"and in the fullness of time she acted upon it." That the whole matter turned out as well as it did is a tribute both to Leonard's basic worth as a person, despite his superficial layer of grubbiness, and the real perceptiveness of the Schlegel girls, whose lives are, after all, dedicated to "personal relations."

Comment

In this chapter we are reminded, in case we had forgotten, that the social balance of the Schlegels and Wilcoxes, "thinkers" and "doers," rests on a very solid foundation of lower middle-class "strivers" - the struggling "have-nots" like Leonard Bast, who are always striving for at least a hint of the glamour with which they imbue the world of the "haves." But Leonard Bast, for Margaret and Helen, anyway, has his own special attractions: a genuine, if already half-crushed sense of romance and a desire to "connect" with life which even the better endowed Wilcoxes, less sensitive by nature, seem to lack.

CHAPTER FIFTEEN

The sisters go out to a kind of combination ladies' discussion club and dinner party after their meeting with Leonard, "full of their adventure" with the strange, pathetic young man. When a paper is read during the evening on the subject of "How ought I to dispose of my money?" - the reader professing to be a millionaire on the point of death-Margaret interrupts the various do-good suggestions with a revolutionary idea of her own: give it to Leonard Bast, or to Leonard Bast and those like him. "whatever you've got, I order you to give as many poor men as you can three hundred a year each." Her listeners object that she'd be "pauperizing them," making them into beggars, putting them, as it were, "on welfare," to use our contemporary terminology. But Margaret replies that a decent income doesn't pauperize a man, it educates him. "Give them a chance," she exclaims. "Give them money. Don't dole them out poetry-books and railway-tickets like babies. Give them the wherewithal to buy these things . . . give people cash, for it is the wrap of civilization, whatever the woof may be." Though she has some trouble converting others to her point of view, the meeting remains friendly, and she and Helen leave in good spirits.

On the way home they chance to meet their old friend, Mr. Wilcox. Chatting idly about this and that, they happen to mention Leonard Bast, and that the young clerk works for the Porphyrion Fire Insurance Company. Always the man of business, Mr. Wilcox is totally uninterested in the plight of Leonard Bast, but he does mention that Porphyrion is about to go under financially. "Let your young friend clear out of Porphyrion Fire Insurance Company with all possible speed," are his exact words.

After some talk about this, Margaret inquires about Howards End, and learns that it has been "let" to an invalid tenant, as the family no longer finds it convenient or comfortable. Margaret is saddened by all this, and after Mr. Wilcox leaves, Helen remarks that he is certainly "a prosperous vulgarian." Nevertheless, the sisters decide to relay his advice to Leonard Bast at once, by asking the young man to tea, though the three had earlier resolved not to meet again.

Comment

Margaret's meeting with Mr. Wilcox in this chapter, and his casual (and as it turns out rather irresponsible) comment about the Porphyrion Fire Insurance Company, set in motion the chain of dramatic events which leads straight to the **climax** of the book. More important, however, this chapter directly states one of Forster's main points in *Howards End*-the obvious-sounding but really rather subtle point that money, and money alone, might be the salvation of such as Leonard Bast. Lending libraries, museums, free schools-all have a place in the upgrading of the poor and deprived, Forster says, but in the last analysis only a substantial personal income can give a man the education, taste and spiritual independence that he needs to become fully mature and developed as a person. Without it, he must remain forever on the grubby treadmill of the white-collar wage-slave, forever barred from the leisure and luxury needed to acquire taste and culture, to devote himself to "personal relations." With it, he has at least a chance, though certainly not a guarantee, of success in the truest sense of the word, spiritual success.

All this is, of course, very reminiscent of the theories of the late nineteenth-century novelist and essayist, Samuel Butler, expressed in *The Way of All Flesh*, and of the ideas of George Bernard Shaw's Andrew Undershaft in *Major Barbara*. Though it may seem crassly materialistic to say so, Butler and Shaw contended, money is often the key to personal fulfillment in our society, and the best things in life are generally not free. Love, relationship, spiritual aspirations-in *Howards End* these are denied to Leonard Bast because of his lack of money. And similarly in *The Way of All Flesh* Ernest Pontifex finds that the poor are much less pleasant and rather less noble than the rich, chiefly because the means to charm and nobility have been lacking in their lives. Though this may seem obvious to us in these days of social work and sociology, we ought to remember that Butler, Shaw and Forster were writing at a time when the poor were all too often sentimentalized, patronized, and shoved out of sight.

CHAPTER SIXTEEN

In order to warn Leonard about the forthcoming failure of the Porphyrion Fire Insurance Company, the Schlegel sisters invite him to tea, and as the perceptive clerk had predicted, his return visit to them is a failure. "As a ladies" lap dog, Leonard did not excel."

As a tea-time guest, he is rather vulgar, with a flat, Cockney sense of humour, and more than a little dull. When the conversation gets around to the company, he indicates clearly enough that he resents what seems to be upper-class interference in his business.

The Schlegels are for "romance," in his scheme of things, not for financial advice. Moreover, naturally suspicious, he imagines they are "picking his brain" to find out Porphyrion secrets! When Mr. Wilcox and his daughter Evie unexpectedly call during the tea, he starts to leave with alacrity, but before he goes, rather an ugly scene develops, in which he accuses the Schlegels of meddling and "brain-picking" and they strenuously defend themselves.

Mr. Wilcox is quite shocked by the whole affair with Bast and tells the sisters that they have no business entertaining a man "of that sort." Margaret tries to describe something of his background-his desire to improve himself, his night-long walk in the country, etc. - but the Wilcoxes' only response is suspicion, a kind of suspicion rather similar to Leonard's. They don't believe he'd walked in the country all night, and they tell Margaret so with many sly innuendos. Suddenly Margaret realizes that Mr. Wilcox is rather jealous of her interest in the pathetic Leonard Bast! "A woman and two men-they had formed the magic triangle of sex, and the male was thrilled to jealousy, in case the female was attracted by another male."

Comment

In this chapter we receive our first hint that the rather causal relationship between Margaret and Mr. Wilcox may develop into something more. Mr. Wilcox is not only protective of the girls in this unfortunate collision of theirs with the lower-class, he is also jealous of Margaret's interest in Leonard Bast. His jealousy is, in fact, as Margaret sees, a result of his essentially "uncivilized" nature, his persistent choice of activity rather than civilization.

But Mr. Wilcox is not the only "uncivilized" individual in this chapter. The limitations of Leonard Bast-his narrowmindedness, suspicion, and vulgarity - are also depicted here. But, of course, there is more excuse for his behavior, at least in Margaret's view. Since no one has ever shown any interest in him before, he simply cannot imagine that anyone ever could want to help him for his own sake!

CHAPTER SEVENTEEN

Time passes and still Margaret has not found a new home. One day when she is most depressed, she receives a note from Evie Wilcox, who has recently become engaged to a Mr. Percy Cahill, The uncle of Charles' wife Dolly, asking her to lunch with them at Simpson's in the Strand, a traditionally "Old English" restaurant favored by active men of the empire-building variety and rather scorned by intellectuals. Margaret has never been there and accepts with some qualms, especially since she doesn't feel she has much in common with the rather mindless, dog-loving Evie or her fiancé. She is pleased, however, to find Mr. Wilcox is of the party. Their conversation touches on a wide range of topics - from house-hunting to theosophy, the near East, socialism and the lower classes - and by the end of the meal they feel much closer than before and agree to see each other again.

Comment

The Wilcoxes' choice of Simpson's as a restaurant - and Margaret's ignorance of the place and its menu-emphasizes their position in the mainstream of British imperialism and her position outside that stream in the quieter, more intellectual backwaters of art and literature, where people eat in health food restaurants and discuss each other's astral planes. Moreover, Margaret's growing attraction to the unintellectual Mr. Wilcox is meant to emphasize what seems to be her growing recognition that the two types, intellectuals and empire-builders, are more dependent on each other than they may think.

CHAPTER EIGHTEEN

Discouraged and disappointed by her failure to find a house, Margaret leaves with Tibby and Helen for a brief vacation at Aunt Juley's house in Swanage, a seaside town several miles from London. One morning, when the family is seated at breakfast, she receives a "businesslike" letter from Mr. Wilcox, offering to rent her his London house on a yearly basis; he no longer wishes to live there, since Evie's engagement, naturally has thought of the Schlegels' need for a new home, and suggests that Margaret come up to London at once to discuss the whole matter with him. But something about the letter makes Margaret think there is more to it than a simple business proposition; she suspects that Mr. Wilcox may in fact be on the point of proposing marriage to her. Indeed, the more she tries to tell herself that her suspicion is a ridiculous "old maid's" fancy, the more convinced she becomes. Nevertheless, she goes up to London prepared for no more than a session of house-viewing and rent-arranging.

Mr. Wilcox himself meets her at Waterloo Station, and he does seem to be behaving rather strangely; he is sensitive, jumpy, and quick to take offense. They go directly to the house, which Margaret finds to be a comfortable, lavishly decorated place, whose heavy, rather vulgar furniture is not exactly to her own, sparer, more ascetic taste. Still, she finds the deep comfort of the large maroon leather chairs -"as though a motor car had spawned" - something of a relief after the delicately aesthetic chairs she is used to, and the whole effect reminds her oddly of an old baronial hall.

In the midst of all this, as the two are settling down seriously to discuss the terms for a lease, Mr. Wilcox does, as Margaret had half-expected, suddenly propose marriage, though with characteristic restraint. Pretending a surprise she doesn't feel, Margaret has time to examine what she does feel - "a kind of central radiance" which must be love. And though she promises to let Mr. Wilcox have her decision as soon as possible after thinking things over, it is clear enough to the reader from her profound happiness and her sense that this is at last the real thing, "the big machinery," that she can give her phlegmatic lover only one reply.

Comment

The romance between Henry Wilcox and Margaret Schlegel has been called the least convincing development in the book by many critics. And indeed, though much has been made of Margaret's attraction to this athletic, energetic, middle-aged industrialist, it is rather hard to believe in the "central radiance" of her feeling for him. Theoretically, in Forster's philosophic scheme, the two- as symbols of the two aspects of England-must fall in love and marry, in order to really show the interdependence of activity and civilization, but it must be admitted that their romance is not very true to life. Mr. Wilcox is so obviously not Margaret's type, and Margaret is so patently being "broadminded" about his spiritual failures that the reader is probably more irritated than pleased by this turn of the plot.

CHAPTER NINETEEN

Aunt Juley and Helen are showing cousin Frieda, now married to Herr Liesecke, around Swanage when Margaret's train appears around a bend, bringing her back from London with her news. Soon she herself arrives in the pony cart with Tibby, who has gone to pick her up at the station. As the party are going in the gate, Margaret whispers to Helen that she has had a proposal from Mr. Wilcox. Helen is first amused, then, when she sees that her sister means to accept, horrified. While everyone else goes into the house, the two stay behind to discuss the matter.

Helen cannot believe that her sensitive, civilized sister Margaret could marry a cloddish character like Mr. Wilcox. She is so upset at the idea, in fact, that she bursts into tears-which in turn upsets Margaret, who thinks Helen is mainly being selfish in not wanting her sister to leave the family. Finally they pull themselves together, however, and Helen seems at least willing to accept the projected marriage. Margaret justifies her strange attraction to the industrialist by explaining on rather theoretical grounds that "If Wilcoxes hadn't worked and died in England for thousands of years, you and I couldn't sit here without having our throats cut... . More and more do I refuse to draw my income and sneer at those who guarantee it." Helen thinks this is all "rubbish" but of course there is little enough she can do about it.

Comment

Helen's bitterness at the idea of Margaret's marriage to Mr. Wilcox foreshadows her intense rebelliousness against the Wilcox world in general, which really begins at this point and increases dramatically from here on. At the same time, Margaret's ability to reconcile herself to the Wilcox lack of imagination and sensitivity still seems rather theoretical.

CHAPTER TWENTY

Margaret duly informs Henry Wilcox that she will marry him, and promptly the next day he arrives at Swanage, "bearing the engagement ring." The two greet each other with "a hearty cordiality" which seems to be typical of many of their exchanges throughout the book, but Margaret reflects that Mr. Wilcox still seems a stranger.

After dinner the engaged pair go for a walk by the sea. Mr. Wilcox wants to discuss "business"; he feels he must explain to Margaret that he has to "do right" by his children, settle a certain income on them, etc., before he marries. Margaret, of course, thinks this only proper and advises her lover to be "generous." "What a mercy it is to have all this money about one!" she exclaims. But Mr. Wilcox deprecatingly replies that she is "marrying a poor man." When she tries to discuss money matters further, more specifically, he puts her off gently: money is not for women to think about.

His protective and rather patronizing attitude toward women comes out in other ways too-when he censures Margaret for a walking tour through the Appenines with her sister, for instance. And his insensitivity is revealed in his admission, now that Margaret is no longer a prospective tenant, that the London house he tried to rent her really had a number of rather serious drawbacks which he had conveniently forgotten to tell her about. Such unconscious dishonesty, says Forster, is "a flaw inherent in the business mind . . ." but, he adds, "Margaret may do well to be tender to it, considering all that the business mind has done for England."

Just before Margaret and Henry part for the night, Henry quite abruptly, with no preparation whatsoever, drops his cigar and kisses her. Margaret is quite startled, and though she responds with genuine love, the incident-so isolated and lacking in tenderness-disappoints and displeases her.

Comment

Henry's perfunctory kiss is characteristic of his patronizing attitude toward Margaret throughout this chapter, and it implies that despite Margaret's optimism, all may not turn out so well with their relationship as she hopes. Henry's dishonesty about the London house and his reticence about business point in the same direction. Perhaps most important, however, is the difference in their attitudes toward money. Margaret thinks herself rich, but Henry, though he is probably richer, regards himself (half humourously, of course) as "poor." "The business mind" of someone like Mr. Wilcox is always striving for more and more money, never concerned about the proper use of money; a "cultured" mind like Margaret's, however, has paused to reflect on the function and purpose of money, without becoming obsessed by the simple accumulation of material goods.

CHAPTER TWENTY-ONE

In this chapter we see Charles and Dolly discussing Mr. Wilcox's impending marriage. Charles, much displeased by the match for a number of reasons, blames his wife for indirectly bringing the engaged couple together-by introducing Evie to her uncle Cahill and thus leaving Mr. Wilcox lonely, at loose ends and, Charles thinks, easy prey for a fortune hunter like Margaret Schlegel! Though he can, of course, do nothing to break up the engagement, Charles resolves to keep a hawk's eye on "these Schlegels" and "if I find them giving themselves airs, or monopolizing my father, or at all ill-treating him, or worrying him with their artistic beastliness, I intend to put my foot down, yes, firmly."

Comment

We see Charles and Dolly talking on their lawn, surrounded by their offspring-one a toddler, one in a pram, and one soon to be born. They are typical, solid, middle-class citizens, the sort, unlike Helen and Margaret, who marry and reproduce early and vigorously. "Nature is turning out Wilcoxes," not Schlegels, "in this peaceful abode," says Forster, "so that they may inherit the earth."

CHAPTER TWENTY-TWO

Back at Swanage, Margaret is hoping to help Henry Wilcox "to the building of the rainbow bridge which should connect the prose in us with the passion" - that is, she is hoping to educate him to greater spiritual freedom and perceptiveness. He tends to be so "obtuse," however - so uninterested in the feelings and problems of others-that she hasn't much chance of succeeding.

One morning Helen receives a letter from Leonard Bast, telling her that, because of Mr. Wilcox's advice, he has given up his job at the Porphyrion Fire Insurance Company and taken a lower paying one in a bank. Helen and Margaret ask Mr. Wilcox if he approves of this step, but he remarks absently that now that it has gotten into the tariff ring, the Porphyrion is a very safe and solid business. Helen, in particular, is appalled and taxes Mr. Wilcox with having caused the poor young clerk to become even poorer. Mr. Wilcox, however, denies that the rich can ever be responsible for the poverty of the poor. "It's part of the battle of life," he explains, rather smugly, and adds that "as civilization moves forward, the shoe is bound to pinch in places." Helen is horrified by this attitude, and Margaret, thinking that "there might at any minute be a real explosion," decides to motor down to Howards End, where there has been some trouble about the tenant, with Mr. Wilcox, in order to get him away from her sister, whose "nerves were exasperated by the unlucky Bast business beyond the bounds of politeness."

Comment

This latest development in the Leonard Bast plot brings us one ominous step closer to the book's tragic **denouement**, a denouement in which both Helen's almost fanatical sense of responsibility and sympathy for Bast's misfortunes, and Henry's thick-headed indifference to the young clerk's plight, will play a part.

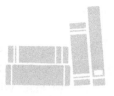

HOWARDS END

CHAPTER TWENTY-THREE

Before Margaret and Henry leave Swanage for their visit to Howards End, Margaret has a talk with her sister Helen. Though Helen insists that she will always dislike Henry Wilcox, she promises at least to be civil to him, and Margaret, in turn, promises to "do what she can" with Helen's friends. The two are able to be completely honest with each other, for, as Forster remarks, "there are moments when the inner life actually 'pays,' when years of self-scrutiny, conducted for no ulterior motive, are suddenly of practical use."

The next day Margaret and Helen motor down from London to Howards End. The house is empty, its tenant having "decamped" without notice, and Margaret is, of course, most anxious to see it after all these years. First, however, they must lunch with Dolly, for Dolly and Charles have taken a house of their own in a nearby suburb. By the time Margaret and Henry get to Howards End, rain is pouring down. Henry discovers that he has forgotten the key, and leaves Margaret on the porch to wait for him while he goes to call for it at the farm down the road, where the caretaker lives. For a few moments she stands on the porch, admiring the lush, incredibly fertile garden before her, then, "sighing, she laid her hand upon the door. It opened. The house was not locked up at all."

In some of Forster's loveliest prose, Margaret explores the house, discovering its grace, proportion and dignity with delight. From the back, she can see a meadow and a pine wood beyond; the garden is full of flowering cherries and plums. Suddenly she hears a noise which seems like "the heart of the house beating, faintly at first, then loudly, martially." An old woman appears, Miss Avery, the caretaker, who remarks "dryly . . . 'Oh! Well, I took you for Ruth Wilcox'" and then passes abruptly out into the rain.

Comment

In this evocative and central scene Margaret at last begins to come into her "spiritual inheritance" of Howards End. The fact that Miss Avery mistakes her for Mrs. Wilcox (and she will soon be Mrs. Wilcox, after all) is significant, as is the fact that she finds the house open when Henry had thought it was locked. Of course *Howards End* represents, in its gracious proportion, what T. S. Eliot (in the *Four Quartets*) calls "the life of significant soil," the orderly tradition of England, in which Margaret, like Ruth Wilcox, will soon take her place.

CHAPTER TWENTY-FOUR

In this chapter Margaret learns more about Miss Avery, the curious, eccentric, old-maid caretaker of Howards End who had so perceptively identified her with Ruth Wilcox the moment she saw her. Back at tea with Dolly, she and Henry talk over the events of the day, and on the way home Margaret meditates further on her trip to Howards End, trying to understand the meaning of the lovely house.

Henry, when he finally arrived with the key, had taken her over the property, explaining the history of what "mismanagement" had reduced from a thirty acre farm, potentially a "small park," to a five or six acre patch of land-the house, the garden and the meadow beyond. To him, Howards End, with all its beauty and tradition, represents little more than a business failure. Yet even so, Margaret thinks, he had saved it from total ruin, without any "fine feelings" or insight, but simply because he is a man who does things - "and she loved him for the deed."

At last she remembers the old wych-elm which guards the house with such dignity, and which Mrs. Wilcox had loved so deeply. Forster has elsewhere (in a *Paris Review* interview) identified the tree as a kind of "genius of the place." Here he remarks that "It was neither warrior, nor lover, nor god.... It was a comrade, bending over the house, strength and adventure in its roots, but in its utmost fingers tenderness.... House and tree transcended any **similes** of sex.... Yet they kept within limits of the human. Their message was not of eternity, but of hope on this side of the grave."

Comment

This chapter continues the definition, begun in the previous one, of a "life of significant soil." "Hope on this side of the grave" is the product of orderly traditions sensitively perceived and graciously respected, a task which only such warm and balanced spirits as Margaret and Ruth Wilcox can carry out, in Forster's opinion. Neither with the "pure" intellectuals nor with the "solid" men of action should the future of England lie, the author seems to be saying, but with those who, like these two extraordinary women, can "build a rainbow bridge between the prose in us and the passion." With whom England's future actually does lie is, of course, another matter, Forster thinks. The selfish, materialistic children of Dolly and Charles, as he pointed out in Chapter Twenty-one, are only too likely to inherit the earth.

CHAPTER TWENTY-FIVE

When Evie hears of her father's engagement to Miss Schlegel, she disapproves quite strongly of it, and, in fact, only forgets her displeasure when the date of her wedding is moved up from September to August; in the intoxication of presents," says Forster dryly, "she recovered much of her good humour."

Margaret, who dislikes most of Henry's "set," is nevertheless, as his future bride, expected to play an important part in this ceremony. In fact, when it is decided that Evie will be married from the present Wilcox country house, Oniton Grange in Shropshire, she is obliged to journey down from London with a party of Henry's most objectionably anti-intellectual and "Public School" circle. Margaret has to admit, however, that the arrangements for the group, however objectionable the individuals may be, have been made by Henry with a deftness characteristic of his wholly practical outlook. Margaret is sure that her own wedding will be either "ramshackly" or "bourgeois" by comparison with this smoothly planned Wilcox bridal.

Margaret is the only Schlegel to attend, of course (Helen and Tibby refuse to go), and she quickly feels out of place among Henry's conventional friends. They are polite and good-humoured, certainly, but thick-skinned and arrogant, also, and their conservative political views are diametrically opposed to her own. When they come to the "astonishing city" of Shrewsbury, for instance, Margaret, perpetually curious, hires a motor car in order to sight-see, while the other ladies and gentlemen linger over tea. Later, as they are being conveyed from the train to the Grange in a special fleet of autos provided by Henry, their car strikes an animal, apparently someone's dog. When Margaret hears a girl crying in a nearby cottage, she tries to find out what has happened. The others, especially Charles Wilcox, who is driving her car, hurry her indifferently on, leaving a servant behind to deal with the girl, whom they suspect of simply wanting money. Margaret, enraged, leaps from the moving car, falls on her knees and cuts her hand. But at this point the servant returns to report that the victim of the accident was just a cat, and Margaret, who can't see why it's being a cat should justify the animal's death, is nevertheless obliged to yield to the group's demands and come away. Later that night she makes light of her experience to Henry, but it has left a deep impression on both her and Charles.

Charles, indeed, will never understand Margaret, for after dinner, as he is sitting outdoors among the picturesque ruins for which Oniton is noted, he sees her climbing toward him and imagines, absurdly, that she wants to seduce him! Margaret, of course, doesn't see him at all. She has only come out to admire what she believes will be her new home. Like Ruth Wilcox, she cares about roots, and imagining that she can put down roots here at Oniton, she has already conceived an affection for the obscure little country town. She little realizes that Henry Wilcox, part of a new rootless "civilization of luggage" and motorcars, has already resolved to leave the place. Nor can she know that the self-righteous Charles believes that she "means mischief."

Comment

Nowhere is the contrast between Wilcoxes and Schlegels more vividly expressed than in this chapter. Margaret's deep personal concern for the girl whose cat has been killed is set against the Wilcox party's casual, almost brutal, indifference to the girl's suffering, and their Bast-like suspicion that she only wants money. Her intellectual curiosity, represented by her sight-seeing at Shrewsbury, is set against their apathy. And finally, her desire for roots, her longing for a real home, a real tradition, is set against what we have already been told is Henry's plan to "let" Oniton Grange, as he has already "let" his London home and Howards End, as soon as possible. The Wilcoxes are perpetually cutting themselves off from the past, even the recent past, just as they cut themselves off from ideas and people; Margaret, on the other hand, is always trying to connect, to relate to places, people, thoughts and traditions. Indifference, isolation, and the "panic and emptiness" which these imply, are the sure accompaniments of the Wilcoxes' outer life of telegrams and anger, while connection and relationship, Forster shows, proceed only from an inner life as deep and vivid as Margaret's and Ruth Wilcox's.

CHAPTER TWENTY-SIX

The next day is Evie's wedding day and the whole Wilcox family is up and about Oniton Grange bright and early. Margaret, fascinated by the place's "romantic tension," wants to go for a walk, but Charles and a friend - clad from head to toe in "indigo blue" - are bathing, with much fanfare, in the nearby river, and would be shocked if she intruded. Upstairs, Evie and her friends are screaming with laughter, playing practical jokes to cover up their nervousness. Only Henry "successfully" dodges emotion, impassively eating his breakfast. "Henry treated a marriage like a funeral, item by item, never raising his eyes to the whole, and 'Death, where is thy sting? Love, where is thy victory?' one would exclaim at the close," is Forster's comment. And Henry's rather chilling reserve does remind us of his behavior at his wife's death and after.

The wedding itself goes reasonably well, though Margaret wishes her own wedding will be "something better than this blend of Sunday church and fox-hunting" which the Wilcox ceremony followed by a garden party wedding breakfast suggests. Soon the bride and groom drive off "yelling with laughter," for Evie is typically insensitive to what properly should be the traditional ceremony and solemnity of a wedding day. Margaret and Henry, left alone, discuss plans for their own forthcoming nuptial. Henry, practical-minded, thinks a hotel ceremony might be best - again a typical, anti-traditional touch.

Suddenly, as Margaret and Henry are standing idly on the lawn, they notice some new guests have appeared - none other than Helen and the Basts! Margaret's rather fanatical younger sister is in a fury, but understandably so, since she claims to have found the young clerk and his frowsy wife "starving" -starving because Leonard, having given up his old job at the Porphyrion, has lost his new one in the bank. Of course she blames Mr. Wilcox for the whole affair, and has come to confront him with the result of his careless remarks; and of course Margaret is torn between anger at her sister's rashness, sympathy for the unfortunate Basts, and a desire not to upset her fiancé, especially on his daughter's wedding day. She offers Leonard and Jacky some food (though Helen has already fed the "starving" pair on the train out) and goes off to try to break the news to Henry as diplomatically as possible. He remembers nothing about the Basts and she prudently doesn't remind him of his disastrous meeting with Leonard at the Wickham Place tea, but she does manage to get him to promise Leonard a job, if he can find one.

When Margaret and Henry come out into the garden together they find that Helen and Leonard have gone away for a moment, and Jacky, apparently drunk, is wandering about alone. Strangely, she calls Mr. Wilcox by his first name and seems to know him well. Suddenly Margaret realizes from Mrs. Bast's remarks that the frowsy woman had once been her upright fiancé's mistress! Shocked, she says nothing, but Henry-certain that she had brought about the whole meeting in order to confront him with Jacky, the evidence of his past misdeeds-melodramatically releases her from her engagement, although as she discovers, the affair had taken place ten years before, and the "tragedy" was therefore not hers, but Ruth Wilcox's.

Comment

This is another very important chapter, especially so because of the **climax** to which the plot line rises. The three different elements of which the story is composed-Basts, Schlegels and Wilcoxes - are all brought together here and dramatically massed against each other, as it were, so that the reader can see the precise way in which they interact: the Wilcoxes ruining both the Basts; and the Schlegels, attracted to the Wilcoxes and sympathizing with the Basts, caught in the middle.

CHAPTER TWENTY-SEVEN

Back at the hotel to which Margaret has sent them, Helen and Leonard Bast are talking things over. Helen knows nothing of the latest development between Mr. Wilcox and Jacky at Oniton Grange, for Leonard has put his intoxicated wife to bed by himself and communicated nothing of the unpleasant truth she told him to his idealistic patroness. The two are still hopeful that Margaret may be able to get Leonard a job with Mr. Wilcox, and while they wait for some word from her, they are having a long philosophical talk about Leonard's life, his marriage, and "Life and Death" in general. Leonard admires Helen enormously-is half in love with her really - and Helen, for her part, is filled with a profound sympathy for the lonely, crushed young clerk. As she talks on-trying to explain to the doubtful Leonard "the emptiness of Money" and the significance of "Death" - he has "the sense of great things sweeping out of the shrouded night. But he could not receive them, because his heart was still full of little things. As the lost umbrella had spoilt the concert at Queen's Hall, so the lost situation was obscuring the diviner harmonies now." Helen's excitement grows as she tries to "cut the rope that fastened Leonard to the earth," but "woven of bitter experience, it resisted her." Presently a waitress enters with a note from Margaret, cutting their conversation short.

Comment

The centrality of money is this chapter's main subject, as it is generally a subject of the sections of *Howards End* having to do with Leonard Bast. The Butler-Shaw-Margaret Schlegel position that money is essential to a full life is shown to be the right one, while Helen's idealistic view that money is "empty" ironically means nothing to her listener, Leonard Bast, whose whole life is being blighted by the lack of it.

CHAPTER TWENTY-EIGHT

While Helen and Leonard are talking at the hotel, Margaret is composing three notes, one to Henry, one to Leonard, and one to her sister. She tells Henry that the unfortunate affair with Jacky is "not to part us . . . It happened long before we met, and even if it had happened since, I should be writing the same I hope." She curtly tells Leonard Bast that Mr. Wilcox "has no vacancy for you," and she tells Helen that "the Basts are not at all the type we should trouble about," and suggests that her sister come at once to Oniton Grange, to spend the night.

Unable to find a servant to carry her message, she delivers the notes to the hotel herself. On the way home she meets Henry and tells him that Helen will probably be coming for the night. Their conversation is cold but polite. "They had behaved as if nothing had happened, and her deepest instincts told her this was wrong."

Comment

Margaret's actions in this chapter-whether right or wrong - are all directed toward the salvation of Henry Wilcox, and of her relationship with him. Forster wants us to believe that she is genuinely in love with the man, and that in her view he "must be forgiven, and made better by love; nothing else mattered," not even the plight of the Basts, about which she might, and might not, be able to do something later.

CHAPTER TWENTY-NINE

At breakfast, Margaret and Henry work out their differences and are soon reunited. Henry "swaggers" about "tragically" before accepting his fiancée's forgiveness, but after he has explained how the whole Jacky affair had taken place ten years before when he was feeling lonely on business in a garrison town on Cyprus, their engagement is quite equably resumed, and they begin to discuss the best way to handle the bothersome Basts.

Margaret is disquieted when she hears that Helen and the Basts have left the hotel separately that morning, without answering either of her notes. "I don't like to think what it all means," she remarks. Mr. Wilcox, who fears blackmail from the Basts, makes her promise never to mention Jacky again; by now he has almost convinced himself that the whole sordid affair never took place at all.

Later on that day, Margaret and Henry leave Oniton Grange, never to return, though Margaret doesn't know it. The Wilcoxes, who have never learned to put down roots, "have swept into the valley and swept out of it, leaving a little dust, and a little money behind," Forster contemptuously says.

Comment

This chapter is most notable for its portrait of the smug Henry Wilcox who, with his lack of self-knowledge, can be melodramatically posturing about his sins one moment, and totally oblivious to them the next, rather self-righteously worrying about the possibility of blackmail.

CHAPTER THIRTY

Now the scene changes to Tibby's rooms at Oxford, several days after the Oniton disaster. Helen, preceded by a telegram, appears with an odd appeal for help from her generally rather indifferent brother. Over lunch, trying to explain her problem, she bursts into tears, then tells Tibby the whole story of Mr. Wilcox's affair and Margaret's cold rejection of Leonard, for which she blames Mr. Wilcox. Tibby thinks it is "a bad business" but can't imagine what is to be done. Helen, however, confides that she has decided to deed a good part of her capital-five thousand pounds, in fact-to Leonard Bast. Tibby is shocked, but she insists on taking the step, as compensation for the wrongs she feels that she and Margaret, at Mr. Wilcox's prompting, have brought on the poor clerk. At last Tibby can only promise to carry out her instructions-first, to do "something" (it is not clear what) about Mr. Wilcox and Jacky second, to forward the money anonymously to Leonard Bast as soon as possible.

The next day Helen leaves the country for Germany, and Tibby informs Margaret, who is much relieved at the news, of her visit. He also sends a cheque to Leonard Bast, who, however, returns it with a "very civil and quiet" refusal, "such an answer as Tibby himself would have given." Though Helen writes Tibby from Germany to keep trying, Leonard Bast persists in refusing her help, and finally the Basts are evicted and move away. Helen reinvests her five thousand pounds after a while and becomes, ironically, "rather richer than she had been before."

Comment

Helen's extravagant and impulsive attempt to do something for Leonard is as much part of her character as Tibby's aloof indifference is of his. Again Tibby is proof that an intellectual can be as lacking in personal warmth and "connectedness" as a man of action like Mr. Wilcox. And Helen seems, at least superficially, to be evidence that all intellectuals are not as reasonable as Margaret seems to be. But later events may, of course, show that Helen's emotionalism is more nearly morally right than her sister's "maturer" rationalism.

HOWARDS END

. . . .

CHAPTER THIRTY-ONE

About two months after Helen leaves for Germany, the Wickham Place house has been torn down and, with the Schlegel furniture temporarily stored at Howards End, Margaret and Henry marry and leave for a honeymoon in Innsbruck. Margaret is hoping to see Helen while they are there, but Helen unaccountably retreats over the border into Italy; Margaret guesses that she is trying to avoid them, but imagines (wrongly) that she wants to do so mainly because of her aversion to Henry.

Oddly matched as they are, the marriage between Margaret and Henry Wilcox seems to be turning out reasonably well. His affection for her grows "steadily," and her tolerant love for him enables her to endure the disappointing discovery that he has rented Oniton Grange to a boy's school because the place is "too damp" and in the "wrong part of Shropshire." Margaret, who now seems to be almost as devoted to the ideal of a permanent home as Ruth Wilcox was, agrees to spend the winter "camping" in Henry's London house, on condition that they really start putting down roots in the spring. Since her marriage, she has lost some of her interest in art, literature and social reform, so she will be glad enough to leave the city for the large country establishment her husband promises her.

Comment

Though Henry and Margaret seem to be forging a happy marriage together, Forster indicates in subtle ways that there is still something rather patronizing about the industrialist's feeling for his wife. He likes her devotion to the arts, for instance, because it "distinguished her from the wives of other men," and he doesn't mind political debates with her because as soon as he grew really serious, she gave in."

CHAPTER THIRTY-TWO

One day the following spring, when Margaret-in London-is looking at plans for the house she and Henry are now planning to build, Charles' wife Dolly bursts in with the strange news that Miss Avery, the eccentric caretaker at Howards End, has been unpacking much of the books and furniture which the Schlegels were storing in the unused house. Charles, Dolly unwittingly indicates, is "very angry" - and evidently he thinks that Margaret may have ordered Miss Avery to take this step, though he doesn't, of course, want to make any accusations. Margaret promises to investigate the matter at once. When she asks Dolly to tell her more about Miss Avery, the girl assures her that the old woman is "dotty," as an example citing a story of Miss Avery's outrage when Evie had abruptly returned her wedding present ("it was too expensive for the old thing"). Margaret, who realizes that the gift must have been given in memory of Ruth Wilcox, is shocked by her step-daughter's rudeness, but Dolly thinks Evie's behavior perfectly reasonable.

The two also discuss Helen's prolonged absence-eight months-in Germany, which is still a source of great concern to Margaret.

Comment

Their rudeness to Miss Avery is typical of the Wilcoxes; as usual, they suspect that she must want something from them-in this case, an invitation to Oniton. Only Margaret, with her long devotion to personal relations and the inner life, can understand Miss Avery's generosity and be shocked by the Wilcoxes' rebuff of it.

CHAPTER THIRTY-THREE

Margaret decides to go down to Howards End at once to see what Miss Avery has done. She sets out on a beautiful day, a day which is to be her "last of unclouded happiness" for many months. After eluding Dolly and the officious niece with whom Miss Avery lives, she proceeds to Howards End, where she finds that the furniture has indeed been unpacked, and that the old woman-who certainly does sound at least half mad-seems to expect her to be moving in soon. Margaret politely explains that there must be some mistake, for she has no such intention, but Miss Avery replies "Mrs. Wilcox, it has been mistake upon mistake for fifty years. The house is Mrs. Wilcox's, and she would not desire it to stand empty any longer." And before Margaret can begin to properly refute this extraordinary statement, Miss Avery begins to show her through the house, in which the Schlegel furniture seems strangely at home. As they walk about, the two women discuss the Wilcox family and the modern world, among other things. "It certainly is a funny world," Margaret remarks, "but so long as men like my husband and his sons govern it, I think it'll never be a bad one—never really bad." But Miss Avery, who detests all the Wilcoxes (except the two Mrs. Wilcoxes, of course) can only answer, discouragingly, "No, better'n nothing."

Unable to persuade Miss Avery that she has no intention of living at Howards End, Margaret returns to London with an odd prediction ringing in her ears. "A better time is coming now, though you've kept me long enough waiting," Miss Avery has said. "In a couple of weeks I'll see your lights shining through the hedge of an evening." Naturally Margaret doesn't believe this, and she plans to ask Henry to help her find a regular furniture warehouse to which she can immediately have her family's belongings removed.

Comment

This scene with Miss Avery is one of the almost supernatural touches in which Forster delights. As we shall see, Miss Avery's action seems to have been based on some kind of second sight. It is as though those, like Miss Avery and Ruth Wilcox, who live in contact with the "significant soil" of Howards End for any length of time soon learn to penetrate beneath the shell of outer events and sense the ultimate direction in which the currents of the spirit will carry people.

CHAPTER THIRTY-FOUR

Soon after Margaret's trip to Howards End, Aunt Juley falls dangerously ill with pneumonia; it seems certain that she will die, so Tibby and Margaret hurry down to Swanage and telegraph to Germany for Helen to join them there. Before Helen arrives, however, Aunt Juley surprisingly takes a turn for the better, and Margaret-who might have taken the opportunity to lure her elusive sister to Swanage anyway-is compelled by her natural honesty to relay the news to Helen, who is already in London.

Back in London, however, Tibby and Margaret try- but fail - to see Helen. They are becoming increasingly desperate about her strange refusal to see them and have even begun to fear that she is mentally ill. Finally Henry, who is not deterred from plotting by Margaret's kind of honesty, proposes that they capture the girl through a trick. Helen has asked Margaret to tell her the whereabouts of their things so that she can pick up some books while she is in England this week, as she plans to return to the continent almost at once. Henry suggests that Margaret send Helen down to Howards End for her things and wait in the house herself, with a doctor, to find out what is wrong. Margaret at first refuses to participate in such a scheme, but when Tibby finally persuades her that their sister's health is at stake, she is forced to consent to it. Strangely enough, Charles Wilcox doesn't like the idea of Howards End being involved in this. "You may be taking on a bigger business than you reckon," he warns his father.

Comment

Henry's unscrupulousness is simply another facet of his business-like "hard-headedness," just as Margaret's principles naturally result from her idealistic devotion to personal relations. She would never sully the trust that is between her and her sister by employing such a deception if she were not frantic with worry by now.

CHAPTER THIRTY-FIVE

The next day, after stopping for lunch with Dolly and her children, Margaret, Henry and a doctor set out for Howards End. Margaret is nervous and repelled by the men's impersonal discussion of Helen's condition. Is the strange girl mad, they wonder, or just high-strung? When they finally arrive at the house, Margaret leaps out of the car and runs up the path ahead of her husband. Helen is already there, and when she rises in an unfamiliar way from her chair on the porch, Margaret realizes the truth at once: her sister is pregnant! In one swift movement she unlocks the door and thrusts Helen into the house, before Henry Wilcox can see her condition for himself.

Comment

Helen's behavior over the past eight months-seeing no one and offering no explanation for her mysterious elusiveness-is now, of course, quite clear.

CHAPTER THIRTY-SIX

Margaret tries to keep the news from Henry and the doctor, but unfortunately they learn the truth about Helen almost at once, by questioning the driver who had brought her from the railway station to Howards End. Henry, or course, is shocked and righteous, but before he has time to express his views any more strongly, Margaret sends him and the doctor away, promising to discuss the matter with them later. She wants only to be alone with her sister now, to hear her story and to beg her forgiveness for the dishonest trick she has played on her.

Comment

In the last analysis, Margaret says, in a situation like this, it is only "affection" that counts. Henry's predictably smug disapproval and shock, and the doctor's professional solicitude, can do nothing for the sisters now.

CHAPTER THIRTY-SEVEN

Left alone, Margaret and Helen are soon reunited. Helen explains that she has been living the Munich with an Italian feminist who has been "much the best person to see me through." They calmly discuss the future, in which they assume that "society." will, of course, see to it that they must be separated because of Helen's misdeed - but they are both inwardly filled with love and regret. After a little while, however, they begin to notice their surroundings: Schlegel furniture carefully arranged throughout Howards End by the indefatigable Miss Avery. It looks wonderful, and in admiring it and exclaiming over the childhood memories individual pieces call up, they soon lose some of their constraint. "Explanations and appeals had failed," Forster explains. "They had tried for a common meeting-ground, and had only made each other unhappy. And all the time their salvation was lying round them-the past sanctifying the present . . . Helen, still smiling, came up to her sister. She said: 'It is always Meg.' They looked into each other's eyes. The inner life had paid.

When a little boy-sent by Miss Avery from the farm-comes to inquire if they want some milk, just as though they are actually settled in to live in the house, Helen gets a wild idea. Wouldn't it be wonderful to spend one night at Howards End, among all their old books and things, before she must leave England for good and they must irrevocably part? Margaret is dubious; she knows Henry will disapprove and Charles will be furious. But she promises, for Helen's sake, to go and ask her husband for his permission at once. "I would have stopped without leave," says Helen, rather crossly, but Margaret insists on asking anyway, and as she drives off, promising to be back by dark, she broods on Miss Avery's remarkable prophecy that they would be living at Howards End within a few weeks.

Comment

Slowly the Schlegel past is merging with the symbolic past of Howards End-one family tradition fusing with what we have come to think of as the spirit of English tradition in general - and already the wonderful house has come to seem a true spiritual refuge to the homeless Helen in her time of need.

CHAPTER THIRTY-EIGHT

Back at Dolly's house Margaret finds Henry intolerably righteous and smug. When he talks pompously about Helen's "seducer" - a subject the more delicate Margaret has not even bothered to ask her sister about - she cannot help thinking that he himself was a "seducer" of Jacky Bast and being appalled by his obtuse double-standard of morality. She asks him if she and Helen may spend the night at Howards End. After some discussion, during which he points out that after all "one thing may lead to another" and they may never get Helen out of the house, he refuses. Margaret is shocked and enraged when he priggishly says "I have my children and the memory of my dead wife to consider. I am sorry, but see that she leaves my house at once." She angrily reminds him of his own affair with Mrs. Bast, as well as of his irresponsible treatment of Leonard. "I've spoilt you long enough," she cries. "No one has ever told you what you are-muddled, criminally muddled." But the insensitive Henry only takes her rebuke as a blackmail attempt and replies that he won't yield to her threats. "I do not give you and your sister leave to sleep at Howards End," he repeats.

Comment

If there was ever any question about Henry Wilcox's character, his appalling behavior at this juncture would settle things at once. His failure to connect his case with Helen's, his smugness, self-righteousness and priggishness all bespeak a sense of morality so primitive and undeveloped that even the loving Margaret can no longer forgive and forget.

CHAPTER THIRTY-NINE

Meanwhile, in London, Charles and Tibby have been informed of Helen's condition, and they meet at Henry's London house to discuss the matter. Charles, as usual, is filled with hatred for, and suspicion of, the Schlegels; Helen, especially, he views as "the family foe." Tibby, as usual, has "no opinions." Unlike Charles, he doesn't care about social **conventions** and only wants, in his rather indifferent way, to see that his sister is all right. When Charles, as obsessed with the identity of the "seducer" as his father, questions Tibby, Tibby mentions almost involuntarily that

Helen had spoken to him at Oxford, before she left for Germany, of "some friends called the Basts." Charles, typically suspicious, immediately jumps to the conclusion that Leonard is the man and that, grotesquely, "you (Tibby) are in his confidence. They met at your rooms. Oh, what a family, what a family!" and he rushes off to relay the news to his father.

Comment

Though Charles is committed to hatred and Tibby is uncommitted to any opinion at all, both are really equally indifferent to Helen's plight. Their reactions are purely social and automatic; Charles' is the usual social rage of his type against anyone who departs from the conventions, and Tibby's is his usual enlightened indifference to the problems of others. The careless way in which he betrays Leonard Bast to the ferocious Charles shows, for instance, how slow he is to perceive the relationships out of which such emotional events are made.

CHAPTER FORTY

Margaret defies her husband and returns to Howards End, to spend the night there with Helen. They spend the evening talking over Helen's situation. The impulsive girl reveals to her sister that Leonard Bast was indeed the father of her child, though he hardly "seduced" her. Rather, she gave herself to him out of pity for him and rage at Mr. Wilcox, on the night of the Oniton Grange disaster. Somehow she felt that her action would make up to the clerk for Henry's seduction of Jacky.

Margaret never reveals to Helen the scene she has just had with her husband, but, tired and lonely as she is, she seems to be drawing strength somehow from the house. It is as though Mrs. Wilcox herself is still guarding them here-the spirit of tenderness and understanding; as though, indeed, as she tells Helen, "you and I and Henry are only fragments of that woman's mind. She knows everything. She is everything. She is the house, and the tree that leans over it. . . . I cannot believe that knowledge such as hers will perish with knowledge such as mine." Just then Miss Avery, who has been working in the house, calls out "Good night Mrs. Wilcox," and we wonder which Mrs. Wilcox she really means. Perhaps Margaret, without knowing it, is growing into the other woman's knowledge. Indeed, though Margaret toys with the idea of accompanying her sister to Germany, especially since her quarrel with Henry, we have a strange feeling that the sisters may have come home to Howards End for good.

Comment

Forster's interest in what might be called the natural supernatural-the way in which spiritual strength may seem to transcend the obstinate materials of life-can be seen in Margaret's words about Mrs. Wilcox in this chapter. He may not really believe that she is a ghost, haunting Howards End, or a godlike mind, understanding all, but figuratively, at least, her radiant personality still endures and dominates the place and the people she once had loved so well.

CHAPTER FORTY-ONE

Now we are returned to Leonard for the first time in many pages. Since the night he spent with Helen at Oniton, the conscientious clerk has been consumed with guilt. "Weeks afterwards, in the midst of other occupations, he would suddenly cry out: 'Brute-you brute, I couldn't have-'. . ." His remorse, indeed, is so intense that it keeps him sleepless, and actually affects his health.

Since he lost his job, furthermore, Leonard has not been able to find another. He has by now been degraded to a "professional beggar," living on handouts from his family. Strangely, amidst all this horror one of the few bright spots in his life is his affection for Jacky; learning the truth about her and Henry Wilcox has only intensified his sympathy for that pitiful woman, and in the end it is for her that he begs. Without her, Forster tells us, "he would have flickered out and died."

One day shortly before Margaret and Henry are to leave for Howards End to trap Helen, Leonard sees Margaret and Tibby at St. Paul's Cathedral. He doesn't speak to them, but they reawaken all his concern about Helen. The next morning he goes to call on Margaret and is told that she has just left for Howards End. After a night of agonized, remorseful insomnia, he too sets out for Howards End, to find Margaret. Arriving at the house, he discovers Margaret, Charles and Helen in the midst of a discussion. When Charles sees Leonard, and learns who he is, he sets out to "thrash" him soundly, hitting him over the head with the first thing that comes to hand-the Schlegel family sword, which Miss Avery had hung over the fireplace. But Leonard, whose health was impaired by the strain of recent events, has a bad heart, and as he grabs for a bookcase to retain his balance, he falls dead of heart failure. The Schlegel books shower down on him as he collapses, and Miss Avery, rushing out of the house, knows at once that "murder" has been committed.

Comment

As if the Wilcoxes have not already done enough to Leonard Bast, they are finally responsible for his death. But significantly, though the Schlegels have wanted only to help the poor clerk, it is with their family sword that the outrageous act has been committed by the bullying, self-righteous Charles Wilcox, and it is the Schlegel books which Leonard grabs at to save himself, but which he only succeeds in pulling down from their shelves in a great, bulky shower of meaninglessness that half buries him as he falls. The entire scene is a symbolic one, after all, representing the obliteration of poor Leonard and his aspirations by the hostile indifference of the industrialists and the bungling interference of the intellectuals.

CHAPTER FORTY-TWO

Charles, we learn, had left London the night before and gone home to Dolly and his father at his own house near Howards End. There he learned that Helen and Margaret were probably defying Henry and staying as Howards End, a fact which enrages his father. "To my mind," storms Henry, "this question is connected with . . . the rights of property. . . ." Charles promises to go and "evict" the Schlegels at eight the next morning, but without violence, of course. And he had been in the process of doing so when Leonard made his unfortunate entrance.

After Leonard's death, Charles returns home to tell his father what has happened. He is unconcerned about his share in the death, since it was obviously due to heart disease. "It did not seem to him that he had used violence . . . even Miss Avery had acknowledged that he only used the flat of the sword," Forster informs us ironically. His father, however, is much more apprehensive. After breakfast he goes round to the police station to inquire about the matter and returns with the news that there is to be an inquest the next day, which Charles is required to attend. "I expected that," says Charles unworriedly, "I shall naturally be the most important witness there."

Comment

Charles' utter lack of feeling for Leonard's death, the total absence of a sense of responsibility for it on his part, emphasizes once and for all the complete obtuseness and disconnectedness of the Wilcox way of thinking. Even Mr. Wilcox is worried, after all, yet the apoplectic bully Charles has so little respect for human life that Bast's death, even his own share in it, is a matter of total indifference to him.

CHAPTER FORTY-THREE

Charles' part in the death may be a matter of indifference to him, but it is not to the police. Margaret and Helen do not understand why they are being questioned so closely about the morning's events, but the reader does. Margaret, however, is more occupied with her plans for the future. Since she has received no apology from Henry, she is determined to go to Germany with Helen. When he comes to see her just before the inquest, she tells him so-then is surprised at his strangeness. Wearier and gentler than usual, he asks her "Have you realized what the verdict at the inquest will be?" "Yes, heart disease." "No, my dear; manslaughter."

And so it is. Charles is convicted of manslaughter and sentenced to three years in prison. Henry is a broken man, and Margaret takes him down to Howards End to recover from the shock.

Comment

The law, Forster says, it "made in Charles' image" - that is, it is vengeful like Charles, and though Leonard Bast might have died of any shock at any time in his condition, the fact that Charles, without intending to murder him, administered the shock that killed, convicts Charles of manslaughter. Henry cannot stand up to this blow; in the end the practical man is not as strong as the idealistic woman. When the outer life of telegrams and anger crumbles, we see once more that the inner life "pays."

CHAPTER FORTY-FOUR

This last chapter takes place fourteen months after Leonard's death. Helen's baby is now a healthy boy of a year, and we discover that she and he are living with Margaret and Henry at Howards End. Miss Avery's prediction has come true. On this particular day, a beautiful summer day, the hay on the big meadow is being cut. Margaret and Helen are sitting outside watching, but Henry Wilcox, and Dolly, Paul and Evie, who have come to visit him, are, of course, remaining indoors. All the Wilcoxes still suffer badly from hayfever. While Margaret and Helen muse on the strange movements of their life, a stranger one is taking place in the house. Henry has just completed arrangements to leave Howards End to his wife and all his money to his children, and he is explaining this to them. They are reasonably satisfied with the idea -none of them especially cares for the house - but still we feel that there is something "uncanny" in Margaret's triumph. "She, who had never expected to conquer anyone, had charged straight through these Wilcoxes and broken up their lives." As for her, Henry tells his children that she intends to leave the house to her nephew, the illegitimate child of Helen and Leonard Bast, so the Wilcoxes are defeated by Basts as well as by Schlegels.

Just before leaving, as Margaret and Henry are biding goodbye to their guests at the door, Dolly, always careless, exclaims "It does seem curious that Mrs. Wilcox should have left Margaret Howards End, and yet she gets it after all." And so Margaret learns for the first time of Mrs. Wilcox's disregarded letter. Henry "tranquilly" tells her the rest of the story, a story whose mysterious outcome makes Margaret shiver. As they sit talking after the other Wilcoxes have gone, Helen, with her baby and a little neighbor boy, rushes into the house. "'The field's cut!' Helen cried excitedly-'the bid meadow! We've seen to the very end, it'll be such a crop of hay as never!'"

Comment

The return of the **imagery** of hay and hayfever, with which the book opened, reminds us that this story is being worked out against the background of an enduring natural pattern into which Margaret and Helen, Leonard Bast and Mrs. Wilcox fit, and from which the other Wilcoxes have isolated themselves. Thus, gradually and inevitably, the inner life triumphs over the outer, and slowly the will of things turns out to be Ruth Wilcox's will-that Margaret have Howards End, and that she come into her inheritance, which is, in Forster's view, the true English inheritance: not the grubby twentieth-century life of cities and motor cars, of oppressed clerks and selfish industrialists, but the life of tradition, of human order and connection set into natural rhythm, of farms and gardens and trees, of "significant soil."

HOWARDS END

. . . .

Margaret Schlegel

She is twenty-nine when the book opens rational yet "impulsive," intellectual, sensitive, liberal, not especially pretty yet with an inner radiance and joie de vivre that make her deeply attractive to those who know and love her. Through her relationships with Henry, Helen, Mrs. Wilcox and Leonard Bast she provides a kind of bridge, connecting the other, more fragmented characters with each other (see essay questions and answers).

Helen Schlegel

Twenty-one at the outset, more intense and impulsive than her sister. At first half in love with the entire Wilcox family, she soon becomes disillusioned with them and takes up the cause of the Basts with a kind of revolutionary fervor. Her child and Leonard Bast's is destined to inherit the Wilcox's house at Howards End.

Tibby Schlegel

"An intelligent man of sixteen," when the book begins, but "dyspeptic and difficile." Though he is an intellectual, he hasn't got the kind of rich, sympathetic "inner life" that Helen and Margaret have. He lacks their talent for personal relations, tends to be both snobbish and selfish. His hayfever is symptomatic, as in the Wilcoxes', of a more general disjunction between him and the natural world.

Aunt Juley (Mrs. Munt)

A well-intentioned, middle-aged busy-body, very British and patriotic, who lacks her nieces' sensitivity to social nuances and their compassion for the unfortunate. She has a "vein of coarseness" which comes out in her quarrel with Charles Wilcox at the beginning of the book.

Ruth Wilcox (Mrs. Wilcox)

About fifty, a gentle, home-loving wife and mother, who seems vague and "out of focus with daily life" in London, yet is fiercely, passionately, attached to her ancestral house at Howards End. Radiantly beautiful as she trails noiselessly across her beloved lawns, she embodies the central ideal of the book, the "aristocratic" ideal of ancestral tradition and order by which Forster thinks the English ought to live.

Henry Wilcox

A successful industrialist in his fifties, impatient, bullying, suspicious with the lower-classes, but dutifully loyal, practical and polite to members of his own class, especially to his own family. He wants companionship and love, Forster tells us, but the "outer life of telegrams and anger" which he lives, and his general insensitivity to the needs and wants of others, too often prevent him from establishing meaningful personal relations.

Charles Wilcox

Like his father, but worse. Bad-tempered, selfish, suspicious. A bully, a prig and a boor. Yet, in the end, there is something almost pathetic about his self-ignorance. He has killed Leonard Bast - feels no responsibility or sympathy for the dead man - and cannot understand that society will hold him, Charles Wilcox, responsible for his act. At this point his insensitivity has gone so far that he comes to seem almost mad.

Dolly Wilcox

Charles' wife, an empty-headed, fluffy little thing. Her name (Dolly) is the perfect clue to her character.

Evie Wilcox

An athletic, insensitive, dog-loving type. She masks whatever feelings she may have beneath a facade of jokes and wisecracks. The picture of her and her new husband, Percy Cahill, driving off "yelling with laughter" after their wedding, is unforgettable.

Paul Wilcox

Charles' younger brother and a milder edition of Charles. His selfishness and irresponsibility lead him to make advances to Helen at the beginning of the book, but he is soon reacting to the Schlegels in much the same way that his brother does.

Miss Avery

The eccentric spinster caretaker of Howards End. She is devoted to the memory of Mrs. Wilcox and sees in Margaret, before Margaret sees it herself, a kind of reincarnation of the older woman.

Leonard Bast

An impoverished, struggling young clerk, with aspirations toward the kind of culture and style which come so naturally to the Schlegels. Though he has a basic sincerity and sensitiveness which have not been entirely crushed by the squalid surroundings in which he is forced to live, he is also suspicious, narrow-minded and touchy as a result, Forster shows, of his difficult life. Indeed, in many ways his suspicion and narrow-mindedness are reminiscent of the suspicion and narrow-mindedness of his social opposites, the Wilcoxes.

Jacky Bast

Leonard's thirty-three year old wife (twelve years older than her husband) and Henry Wilcox's former mistress. An overblown, frowsy type with a good heart. To Margaret - and to Leonard too, really, -she seems pathetic; like Leonard, she has been crushed by life, denied any opportunity to develop herself into the more civilized person she might have been in a different social environment.

A PASSAGE TO INDIA

....

A Passage to India is divided into three long sections, which correspond, according to Forster, to the three seasons of the Indian year-Mosque (the cool weather), Caves (the hot weather), and Temple (the rains).

CHAPTER ONE

This first chapter of the Mosque section is a description of Chandrapore, an undistinguished, medium-sized, Indian city located on the river Ganges. Just outside the city proper, on a slight elevation above it, is the British colony, consisting of a brick clubhouse and a group of bungalows where members of the Indian civil service live, as far as possible from the natives. Though Chandrapore has many gardens and a few fine houses, Forster tells us, it is essentially "meagre" and "monotonous." Its only unusual geographical feature is the Marabar Hills, which contain "the extraordinary caves." And only the sky can rain "glory" onto the insignificant little town, because over this endless, prostrate Indian plain only the sky is "so strong and so enormous."

Comment

Forster introduces some of the book's central **imagery** in this first brief chapter-the mysteriously changing, all-controlling sky of India; the endless, seemingly meaningless Indian plain; the "meagre," impoverished city, so shapeless and "muddled" to western eyes; and the "sensibly planned" British colony, cut off from the rest of the town in location and design; as well as, most important, the "extraordinary" Marabar caves, which will summarize many of Forster's main **themes** in one especially dramatic symbol.

CHAPTER TWO

Dr. Aziz, a young Indian physician, a Moslem, arrives at a dinner party given by his friend Hamidullah, one of the more educated and wealthier Moslems in Chandrapore and the town's leading attorney. Another guest is Mahmoud Ali, also a lawyer. As the three await dinner, they relax on the verandah, smoking hookahs (water pipes) and discussing the failings of their supercilious British rulers. Their special targets are Mr. and Mrs. Turton, the top-ranking Chandrapore official and his wife, and someone they call "Red-Nose," a young English Magistrate who had once been kind to Mahmoud Ali in court but whose liberal ideas were soon lost after a few more months in India. Just before dinner, Hamidullah takes Aziz around to the women's quarter to see his wife, who happens to be a distant relative of the young doctor's. Aziz was left a widower a few years earlier, when his wife died giving birth to their third child, and Hamidullah Begum seizes every opportunity to try to persuade the lonely widower to remarry. Aziz lives by himself in a small, shabby bungalow, sending all his salary to his children who live with their maternal grandmother in another town. Hamidullah Begum believes that her young relative would be happier if the remarried; furthermore, she thinks it is his duty to make some young woman happy too.

After some minutes of this, Aziz and Hamidullah go in to dinner. But their meal is barely on the table when a curt note arrives for Aziz, summoning him to the home of Major Callendar, his superior at the hospital. Furious at the Englishman's rudeness-he doesn't even bother to explain what he needs Aziz for-Aziz rushes off on his bicycle, gets a flat, and finally takes a tonga (a horse-drawn Indian taxi). When he arrives at the house he finds that the Civil Surgeon (Major Callendar) has gone out without leaving a message for him. Worse, Mrs. Callendar and a British friend, Mrs. Lesley, on their way to the Club, cut him and take his tonga without thanks. Angry and depressed, he leaves on foot, planning to walk home.

On his way, however, he passes one of his favorite mosques and stops in for a moment's meditation. Suddenly he sees an Englishwoman moving about among the pillars. Shocked, and still smarting from his encounter with Mrs. Callendar, he reprimands her for not having taken off her shoes, and is even more astonished when she calmly informs him that she already has. "I was right, was I not?" the strange lady asks. "If it removed my shoes, I am allowed?" "Of course," Aziz replies, "but so few ladies take the trouble, especially if thinking no one is there to see." "That makes no difference," she answers, adding, "God is here."

Aziz realizes the woman is extraordinary, though he sees that she is old and whitehaired, not young and beautiful as he would have wished. They introduce themselves; she is Mrs. Moore, the elderly mother of Ronny Heaslop, the British City Magistrate who was Mr. "Red-Nose" in Mahmoud Ali's narrative earlier. Here on a visit, she has left a boring performance of Cousin Kate at the British Club to see India by night. Chattering excitedly-he is now as warm and affectionate as he was angry before-Aziz walks her back to the Club and explains that Indians are not allowed in, when she says that she wishes he could be her guest. "He did not expatiate on his wrongs now, being happy. As he strolled downhill . . . he seemed to own the land as much as anyone owned it. What did it matter if a few flabby Hindus had preceded him there, and a few chilly English succeeded?"

Comment

In this chapter we are introduced to Aziz and Mrs. Moore, two of the four or five main characters in the book. The gulf between Indians and English, which the description of the British colony in chapter one emphasized, is a gulf which both Aziz and Mrs. Moore want to bridge right now, though Aziz, knowing more about the situation, is angrier and less hopeful than the elderly Englishwoman. Their present attitudes will change before the book is over, however, and the chain of events which their first meeting in the darkened mosque sets in motion will change them. Already, furthermore, in the last few lines of the chapter (quoted above) India as a symbol-Hindu, Moslem and British India-is expanding to include, more than national or religious identity, the whole inexplicable universe which man cannot control or comprehend.

CHAPTER THREE

Mrs. Moore returns to the club, where, unable to stand the performance of Cousin Kate, a third-rate British comedy, she sits in another room with Adela Quested, her traveling companion and her son's prospective fiancée. (The main reason for M,s. Moore's trip to India was to chaperone Miss Quested, who can't make up her mind whether or not to marry Ronny and wants to see him "on the job" in India before deciding.) Both women are anxious to see "the real India" and are bored by the dull, parochial round of British tea parties which is all they've seen so far. When Major Turton, Ronny's superior, hears that they want to meet some Indians, he obligingly offers to arrange a "Bridge Party" for them, to which both nationalities will be invited. The other British ladies are amused and faintly shocked that anyone should want to meet Indians, but Mrs. Moore and Adela gratefully accept Mr. Turton's offer.

On the way home, Mrs. Moore mentions her meeting with Aziz at the mosque to her son. He is upset and annoyed at the idea of her talking to a native and reprimands her rather sharply for allowing such "impudence." Later, at home, he pursues the subject; discovering Aziz's identity, he says that the young doctor is all right, but seems ready to report one of his anti-Callendar remarks to the Civil Surgeon himself. Mrs. Moore is annoyed and shocked at this in her turn; her son would never have so rudely betrayed a confidence at home. But "India isn't home" is Ronny's reply, though he finally agrees to keep his knowledge of Aziz to himself for the time being at least.

Later still, when she is about to hang up her cloak, Mrs. Moore notices a wasp sleeping on the peg. The strange image of the insect, impersonally "nesting" in the house as though he is outdoors, seems to symbolize the strangeness of India, where a house becomes almost a part "of the eternal jungle, which alternately produces houses trees, houses trees."

Comment

The grating intolerance of the British toward the Indians is again depicted throughout this chapter; the hostile gulf between the two will, after all, be one of this book's major themes. But the more difficult, less easily explained **theme** of India as "the eternal jungle," eternally mysterious and muddled, at least to the human reason, is also present here, in the incident of the wasp. Slowly Mrs. Moore, who is the most visionary character in the book, especially in comparison to the English and the Moslems, is coming to sense that there is another level on which life exists-a blind yet profound level of life-which must be confronted more often in India than anywhere in the west.

CHAPTER FOUR

Next day the Collector-Mr. Turton-issues invitations to the "Bridge Party." The Indians who receive them are much excited. Some, like Mahmoud Ali, speculate that Mr. Turton has been forced to give the party by "higher ups." Others, like the Nawab Bahadur, a powerful local landowner, are less suspicious of the Englishman's motives. Most, however, no matter what their reaction, decide to attend the gathering.

Comment

Although they are often savagely critical of their British rulers, the Indians-like many subject peoples - are also pathetically grateful for the slightest sign of attention or kindness from them.

CHAPTER FIVE

The "Bridge Party" is definitely not a success. The British, for the most part contemptuous of the Indians, and a little nervous with them too ("It's enough to make the old type of Burra Sahib turn in his grave"), remain aloof, in a little, superior group on one side of the Club lawn; the Indians, most of whom have arrived early, stand "massed at the farther side of the tennis lawn, doing nothing." The gulf between the two groups is a physical as well as a social one.

Finally Mr. Turton arrives and forces his wife to accompany him across the lawn to the Indian side of the party. But their greetings are cold and perfunctory. Even Mrs. Moore and Miss Quested, with all the good will in the world, cannot get much response from the Indians after this pattern of British frigidity has been established. They ask to call on one of the Indian ladies-Mrs. Bhattacharya - and are met with a bewildering combination of friendliness and ignorance. Only Mr. Fielding, the Principal of the little Local Government College, who is not what the British ladies call a "pukka sahib" "romps" among the Indian guests, "athletic and cheerful . . . making numerous mistakes which the parents of his pupils tried to cover up, for he was popular among them."

Fielding learns that the two new ladies, Adela and Mrs. Moore, are much liked by the Indians, and when he hears of their interest in meeting "real" Indians, he resolves to make a better attempt at introducing them to natives than the dismal "Bridge Party" has been. He, of all the Europeans in Chandrapore, knows enough Indians to do this, so Adela and Mrs. Moore are delighted to accept his invitation to tea. He plans to ask Aziz and a Hindu Professor of music from his College also, for he's heard of Mrs. Moore's meeting with Aziz.

Despite the prospect of Fielding's tea, however, Adela is depressed by the spirit of British India in general-its dull Englishness, conventionality, and smugness. Later that night, Mrs. Moore tries to explain to Ronny what is bothering Adela. He thinks the Indian weather, especially the heat, is the worst there is to bear in British India. But Mrs. Moore says "it's much more the Anglo-Indians themselves who are likely to get on Adela's nerves. She doesn't think they behave pleasantly to Indians, you see." Ronny, surprised, exclaims "how like a woman to worry over a side-issue!" and when his mother objects, he adds "We're not here for the purpose of behaving pleasantly . . . We're out here to do justice and keep peace." Mrs. Moore, however, replies that "the English are out here to be pleasant . . . because India is part of the earth. And God has put us on earth in order to be pleasant to each other. God . . . is . . . love." His mother's argument makes Ronny "gloomy," however. He knows this "religious strain in her" and regards it as a "symptom of bad health."

Comment

This chapter continues to depict the gulf between the British and the Indians, but also, in Mrs. Moore's final conversation with her son, it presents the first of many explorations of the British purpose -and the British practice - in India. Need a ruler, who must get things done amid the chaos of the strange Indian world, treat his subjects "pleasantly?" Or, after all, need a ruler "get things done" at all? What is his ultimate purpose in India anyway? To teach the Indians British ways, or to be instructed by India itself? Mrs. Moore's "religious strain," which her son thinks a symptom of bad health, may actually be a sign of good health - of good spiritual health, which she, of all the characters, possesses in greatest measure. Her dictum that "God . . . is . . . love" reminds us of Margaret Schlegel's motto of "Only connect" in *Howards End*, and Mrs. Moore's vague yet loving personality will increasingly recall Ruth Wilcox in the same book.

CHAPTER SIX

Aziz does not go to the "Bridge Party," though he has been invited and has in fact promised to accompany his colleague, Dr. Panna Lal, in his new tum-tum (a horse-drawn carriage). Aziz has had a row with Major Callendar about his superior's rudeness the night of Hamidullah's dinner-party, and furthermore the party happens to be set for the anniversary of his wife's death.

Though his marriage was an arranged one and he did not at first love his wife (she was not beautiful, apparently), Aziz fell in love with her after the birth of their first child. "He was won by her love for him, by a loyalty that implied something more than submission, and by her efforts to educate herself against that lifting of the purdah that would come in the next generation if not in theirs. She was intelligent, yet had old-fashioned grace."

A combination of laziness and grief keeps Aziz from telling Dr. Panna Lal in time that he isn't going to the party. After brooding for some time that afternoon, however, the young doctor cheers up and goes off to play polo on a field just outside town. A good rider though a bad player, he knocks a ball about for a bit with a British subaltern who happens to be there. The exercise promotes good fellowship and Aziz is annoyed when Dr. Panna Lal happens to pass by on his way back from the party.

He has had trouble with his horse and blames Aziz for not telling him he couldn't come, as he'd counted on him to help control the animal. They end up quarreling, and Aziz later regrets that he impulsively galloped past his timid friend's horse, causing it to bolt once again.

At home, he finds a note waiting for him. He fears that it may be a letter of dismissal from his job because of his failure to attend the "Bridge Party," but it turns out to be only Mr. Fielding's invitation to tea on the coming Thursday.

Comment

Aziz's behavior, alternately hostile toward Englishmen of the Major Callendar type and desperately grateful for the kindness of such a man as Fielding, is inevitable given the situation in India and Aziz's own essential warmth and impulsiveness of character. His selfish behavior to Dr. Panna Lal, like his quickly-forgotten grief for his wife, is only another manifestation of that same impulsiveness.

CHAPTER SEVEN

Mr. Fielding became an Anglo-Indian late-after forty - and perhaps that is one reason for his tolerance, compared to the other members of the British colony. As a rather worldly man near middleage, he wasn't as likely as the callower young men of the Indian civil service to become alarmed by, and consequently prejudiced against, the strangeness and "otherness" of Indian civilization. Now, Forster tells us, Fielding is a "hard-bitten, good-tempered, intelligent fellow . . . with a belief in education . . . The world, he believed, is a globe of men who are trying to reach one another and can but do so by the help of good will plus culture and intelligence-a creed ill-suited to Chandrapore, but he had come out too late to lose it." Fielding did most harm to his reputation among the British by saying one day at the Club that "the so-called white races are really pinko-grey." His male listeners were "subtly scandalized" and their wives decided that Mr. Fielding was "not a sahib really."

Aziz arrives for the party in good spirits, and the two men, who have never met before, become friends immediately. When Fielding accidentally breaks a collar stud Aziz even impulsively lends the Englishman his own. The tea party, moreover, turns out to be "unconventional" but successful, unlike the ill-fated "Bridge Party." Aziz thinks Adela plain, but finds her and Mrs. Moore easy to talk to. And indeed he is a great success-chattering away with a verve that is typical of him when he is well-received by others. The group decide that "India's a muddle . . ." at least Mr. Fielding thinks so, and that it is also a mystery.

In the course of the conversation, Aziz extravagantly invites all the guests to visit him one day (though he doesn't really want anyone to see his shabby bungalow), for it turns out that their promised visit to the Bhattacharyas never materialized. (The Hindu couple seem to have inexplicably forgotten their invitation.)

After Professor Godbole, a quiet, rather enigmatic, very religious and polite Hindu arrives, Aziz calms down somewhat, but the afternoon remains a triumph for him. Only, when Adela seems to be taking up his invitation, he hastily changes it: "I invite you all to see me in the Marabar caves," he says, grateful for a way of keeping the British ladies from his bungalow. Adela asks him to describe the caves, but oddly enough Aziz has never been there himself and cannot do so. The group then encourages the mysterious Professor Godbole to speak about them, but he seems strangely unwilling to. Suddenly Ronny Heaslop arrives to pick up Adela and Mrs. Moore. With typical Anglo-Indian snobbishness he icily cuts Aziz and the Professor, thereby thoroughly puncturing the warm mood of the party. Now everyone is "cross and wretched." Somehow there seems to be "no reserve of tranquillity to draw upon in India. Either none, or else tranquillity swallowed up everything, as it appeared to do for Professor Godbole."

Just before the British group leaves, the enigmatic, calm Professor is persuaded to sing for them. His song is unintelligible to western ears, but the Indian servants seem to appreciate it. Afterwards, he explains it in a key passage: "It was a religious song. I placed myself in the position of a milkmaiden. I say to Shri Krishna, 'Come! come to me only.' The god refuses to come. I grow humble and say: 'Do not come to me only. Multiply yourself into a hundred Krishnas, and let one go to each of my hundred companions, but one, O Lord of the Universe, come to me.' He refuses to come. This is repeated several times . . . 'But he comes in some other song, I hope?' said Mrs. Moore gently. 'Oh no, he refuses to come,' repeated Godbole, perhaps not understanding her question. 'I say to Him, Come, come, come, come, come, come. He neglects to come.'"

Comment

The Marabar caves, a central symbol in the book, are at last introduced into the story's action in this chapter-strangely enough, by Aziz, who knows nothing about them. Professor Godbole, who does know about them, seems to be in possession of other secrets as well-a kind of cosmic tranquillity pervades his acceptance of both social inequities (Ronny Heaslop's intolerably rude snub) and universal emptiness (the god Krishna's failure, in life as in song, to come).

CHAPTER EIGHT

As they leave the party, Adela and Ronny begin to quarrel about Aziz's invitation to the Marabar caves, which the young Englishman thinks thoroughly unsuitable, coming from a native. Adela is quite disappointed in Ronny; India has changed his character for the worse. "His self-complacency, his censoriousness, his lack of subtlety, all grew vivid beneath a tropic sky." Fatigued by their bickering, Mrs. Moore asks to be dropped at the bungalow before the two go on to a polo match.

At the polo match Adela tells Ronny that she cannot marry him. He is naturally disappointed but masks his feelings with typical British reserve. Adela sympathetically remarks that "I know we shall keep friends," and a wave of tenderness sweeps over both, so that when the Nawab Bahadur-also present at the match-invites them for a spin in his new car, they are glad to go off together. They even end up holding hands on the back seat.

As the large, expensive motor car rushes along, however, it suddenly strikes something - an animal, perhaps a hyena, Adela and Ronny speculate. The Nawab Bahadur, though doesn't respond to the situation with such British restraint and practicality. Instead, he becomes intensely - unaccountably -upset. When Miss Derek, a Maharani's British "companion," drives up with her employer's motorcar (which she has taken, without leave, on her vacation) he hastily jumps in, along with Adela and Ronny, abandoning his Eurasian chauffeur, for whom there is no room in the auto, without a second thought.

On their way home, Adela is so moved by her experience in the car with Ronny that she reverses her earlier decision and agrees to marry him. Back at their bungalow, they tell Mrs. Moore the news - and they also tell her about the "accident" in the Nawab Bahadur's car. Her response is strange. She shivers inexplicably and exclaims "A ghost!" But the young people hardly notice.

Meanwhile, at his town house in Chandrapore, the Nawab Bahadur explains the reason for his distress at the incident to some Indian friends, including Dr. Aziz. "Nine years previously, when first he had a car, he had driven it over a drunken man and killed him, and the man had been waiting for him ever since. The Nawab Bahadur was innocent . . . but it was no use, the man continued to wait in an unspeakable form, close to the scene of his death. None of the English people knew of this . . . it was a racial secret communicable more by blood than speech." The impressionable audience shudders and only Aziz-the most enlightened of that company-thinks the old man's belief is no more than "superstition."

Comment

The British restraint of Ronny and Adela contrasts sharply with the impulsiveness and outgoingness of Dr. Aziz. The fact that the lovers (if they can be called that) quarrel about an invitation to the Marabar caves foreshadows the increasingly troublesome role these strange caves will play in the story.

The incident in the Nawab Bahadur's car, and Mrs. Moore's striking, almost clairvoyant interpretation of it, shows that she - and not the skeptical Indian Aziz-is approaching that mystical accord with the universe, that intuitive understanding of its events and implications, which would ordinarily, in Forster's view, seem to be characteristic of the Indians rather than the English. Perhaps, Forster now suggests, one must have a kind of spiritual talent to see to the heart of things, a talent which the wise and religious Mrs. Moore, like Mrs. Wilcox before her, has got, and which the callow Aziz, like Ronny and Adela, lacks as yet. Forster frequently employs these touches of the supernatural - more often in *A Passage to India* than in *Howards End* (where, however, the "mind" of Mrs. Wilcox seems to live in the house and garden long after her death). For him, the supernatural seems to be a dramatic way of representing spiritual strength, strength, like Mrs. Moore's, which reaches beyond the materialistic concerns of men like Ronny-and even Aziz-to the cosmic questions that society all too often ignores.

CHAPTER NINE

Shortly after the tea party at Fielding's, Aziz comes down with a slight fever and decides to treat himself to a day in bed. He lies in his cluttered little bungalow, in the swelling heat, disgusted by the clumps of flies on the ceiling and thinking of beautiful women. After a while a group of his friends arrive to see him, including Hamidullah and a few other educated Indians. There is a rumour abroad that Professor Godbole is also ill-following the tea party - and with cholera. When Aziz's colleague, Dr. Panna Lal, comes in to examine him, the other Indians question him about Godbole, his patient and a fellow Hindu. But it develops that the tranquil professor is not suffering from cholera at all; he merely has hemorrhoids!

Now Mr. Fielding arrives, and since it is most unusual for an Englishman to visit a native in this way, he is greeted very deferentially by Aziz's friends. Aziz himself, however, is ashamed of his shabby bungalow and wishes his new British friend had not come. He remains rather cool and distant, but the rest of the group discuss politics and religion with animation, and then the Indians prepare to go. Fielding, too, takes his leave, but for some reason Aziz's servant fails to bring his horse. As he waits on the porch, disappointed with his call (because Aziz's remoteness), "the Club comment, 'making himself cheap as usual,' passed through his mind."

Comment

The obstacles to British-Indian friendship are numerous, and they include, as we see in this chapter, the Indians' own sense of inferiority and shame at their Indianness. Fielding is trying to bridge the gulf between himself and Aziz, but though Aziz would like to bridge it too, neither can quite rid himself of the embarrassment and resentment which inevitably widen rather than close such a rift.

CHAPTER TEN

Outside of Aziz's bungalow the heat is growing, swelling and "leaping forward" through the street as though it were a living creature. It is April now, "herald of horrors," and as the sun returns to his kingdom "with power but without beauty" the Indian hot weather begins.

Comment

The weather is inextricably involved with the mood of *A Passage to India*, and Forster himself disclosed, in his notes to the

Everyman edition of the book (1942), that he meant the three sections of the novel, Mosque, Caves and Temple, to correspond to the three seasons of the Indian year-the cool, the hot and the rainy. Cool weather, as in Mosque, this first section, is associated with a time of relative sanity and restraint; the heat is connected with irrationality, nightmare, hallucinations and a vision of cosmic disorder; finally, the rains accompany revival and refreshment, a renewal of the earth and of life itself.

CHAPTER ELEVEN

After the other Indians have left, Aziz calls Fielding back into his room, and after some bitter, anti-British talk, surprises the Englishman by showing him a picture of his dead wife. Fielding is extraordinarily complimented by this action, because Aziz is a Moslem whose family observes the Purdah, or seclusion of women from all men except relatives. The two seal their friendship with some talk about Aziz's marriage, and Fielding regrets that he has no comparable way of honoring his Indian friend - no secrets to tell, no confidences to give in exchange. They discuss Englishwomen in general and Miss Quested in particular. Aziz thinks her unattractive and flatchested, but Fielding finds his friend's criticism a bit vulgar. Aziz then reprimands Fielding for his frankness about his religious beliefs - or lack of them-in the conversation earlier. Though the young doctor no longer stands in such awe of the school principal, they are "friends, brothers." Fielding leaves in good spirits and Aziz drops happily off to sleep.

Comment

Fielding and Aziz seem to be well on the way toward cementing a real Anglo-Indian friendship. It remains to be seen, however, how well the relationship can stand up to the extraordinary strain of Indian life-especially of the hot weather.

The discussion of Adela Quested's charms, or lack of them, as well as Aziz's attitude toward his wife and his earlier fantasies about "beautiful women," will begin to seem increasingly significant in the chapters soon to come.

A PASSAGE TO INDIA

. . . .

CHAPTER TWELVE

Here begins the "hot-weather" section of the book, called Caves. Appropriately enough, this chapter is devoted to a description of the Marabar caves-a series of undecorated, twenty-foot chambers with polished walls, each of which is approached by an eight-foot long tunnel with rough walls. They are all exactly alike. "Having seen one such cave," Forster explains, "having seen two . . . the visitor returns to Chandrapore uncertain whether he has had an interesting experience or a dull one or any experience at all. He finds it difficult to discuss the caves, or to keep them apart in his mind, for the pattern never varies, and no carving, not even a bees'-nest or a bat distinguishes one from another . . . One of them is rumoured within the boulder that swings on the summit of the highest of the hills; a bubble-shaped cave that has neither ceiling nor floor, and mirrors its own darkness in every direction infinitely."

Comment

The caves in *A Passage to India* seem to stand for what Helen Schlegel in *Howards End* called the "panic and emptiness" of the universe. Indeed, as Forster uses them, they show a remarkable similarity to many of the images of cosmic insignificance and "absurdity" which are employed by such contemporary existentialists as Samuel Beckett, Jean Paul Sartre and Albert Camus. Bewilderingly blank, meaningless and empty, the Marabar caves represent a universe which man must confront but cannot comprehend, a universe from which God-the orderly principle, the principle of love and life-has withdrawn, or to which, like Krishna in Professor Godbole's song, he "neglects to come." Infinitely multiplied and yet cut off from each other, they are like the souls of men-or perhaps, better, like the lifeless hulks of men-isolated and empty, amid cosmic insignificance.

CHAPTER THIRTEEN

For some time Aziz has forgotten his invitation of Mrs. Moore and Adela to the Marabar caves, but one day a servant overhears Adela wondering aloud about his neglect of them, and this information is relayed to him via the Indian "grapevine." Of course, he strenuously renews the invitations, and despite all kinds of difficulties (everyone eats a different diet, for instance) it is finally settled that Adela and Mrs. Moore will visit the caves with him and Professor Godbole, provided that Mr. Fielding comes along too-as a trustworthy Englishman, to satisfy Ronny that everything is all right.

Finally the great day arrives; the party are to meet at the train, and Aziz is so nervous about lateness that he spends the night at the station in order to be punctual. In the morning Mrs. Moore and Adela arrive in plenty of time for the train, and Aziz helps them into the Purdah car where they are to ride. Suddenly he sees that the gates have been closed unusually early; the train is about to start and Fielding and Godbole have not arrived. Aziz and his friend Muhammad Latif leap aboard, and as the train pulls out of the station they catch sight of Fielding and the professor, who have missed it because Godbole took too long with his prayers.

Aziz is in despair, but Mrs. Moore, always kind and thoughtful, consoles him. Adela too is kind, and finally he cheers up, feeling increasingly "important and competent" on his own. "'Indians are incapable of responsibility,' said the officials . . . He would show those pessimists that they were wrong." But he still doesn't know what is in the Marabar caves, or why they are going to see them.

Comment

Aziz's ignorance about the caves is part of his general ignorance of the universe and the way it works. He is a warmhearted and well-intentioned person, but still rather callow and superficial; as yet he has not penetrated to the "panic and emptiness" which are at the heart of things, and consequently he is not yet mature enough to come to terms with life.

CHAPTER FOURTEEN

On the train, where they are regally pampered by the servants Aziz has hired for the occasion, Adela and Mrs. Moore discuss Adela's forthcoming marriage to Ronny. The couple are to be married in Shimla, in the hills, to escape the heat, and because the wedding won't take place until May, Mrs. Moore, who now wants to return to Ralph and Stella, her children by another marriage, won't be able to leave India till after the hot weather.

The scenery around them is rather dull during most of the journey, but as they approach the Marabar hills, it becomes more spectacular, and a dramatic sunrise raises their hopes. "But at the supreme moment, when night should have died and day lived, nothing occurred. . . . The hues in the east decayed, the hills seemed dimmer though in fact better lit, and a profound disappointment entered with the morning breeze." India-like Professor Godbole's song-leaves everyone and everything strangely unfulfilled.

When they alight at the Marabar station, Adela and Mrs. Moore find that Aziz has hired an elephant to transport the whole party to the caves. After some bustling about by the servants, they get underway, and are served poached eggs and tea as soon as they arrive in the shadow of the hills. (Aziz is under the impression that the English must be fed every two hours!) Buoyed up by the sense that he is succeeding as a host - and proving in the process that a native can be a good host - Aziz feels overwhelmingly fond of Adela and Mrs. Moore. He and Mrs. Moore reminisce about their first meeting in the mosque, and then the tactful woman draws him out on the subject of the earliest Mogul rulers of India, a subject - unlike the caves - about which he knows something.

Adela, too, asks Aziz about India: how shall she behave after her marriage to Ronny? "I am told we all get rude after a year," she says. "Then you are told a lie," Aziz replies quickly, "for she had spoken the truth and it touched him on the raw."

After this brief rest the three visit their first cave, where Mrs. Moore has a terrifying experience. "Crammed with villagers and servants, the circular chamber began to smell. She lost Aziz and Adela in the dark, didn't know who touched her, couldn't breathe, and some vile naked thing struck her face and settled on her mouth like a pad . . . not only did the crush and stench alarm her; there was also a terrifying echo."

When she leaves the cave, Mrs. Moore discovers that "the naked pad was a poor little baby, astride its mother's hip." Nevertheless, she decides not to visit another. She explains that she is feeling unwell, and while Aziz and Adela go on ahead she settles down to write a letter to Ralph and Stella. Her experience in the cave has shaken her considerably, however. It seems as though a voice has told her that "Pathos, piety, courage-they exist, but are identical, and so is filth. Everything exists, nothing has value." The echo in the cave has reduced everything to a meaningless boum. "Motionless with horror" and sick at heart, Mrs. Moore loses in a moment all her joy in life, and all interest, even in Aziz; "the affectionate and sincere words that she had spoken to him seemed no longer hers but the air's."

Comment

In this central chapter, Mrs. Moore has a nihilistic vision of the universe in the Marabar caves which obliterates-or seems to obliterate-her earlier belief that "God . . . is . . . love." Suddenly it seems as though there is no God, and the consequent emptiness and meaninglessness of life become insupportable to her. The "Marabar . . . (had) robbed infinity and eternity of their vastness, the only quality that accommodates them to mankind." And in the process of doing so, it also robs mankind of all dignity; evil seems to be let loose upon the world, and even an innocent child is reduced to a vile and helpless thing, no more than a "naked pad" in the polished darkness of the cave.

CHAPTER FIFTEEN

Adela and Aziz continue on with the guide to the next cave. They have never particularly liked each other, and Adela, especially, is rather bored by the whole expedition and preoccupied with her wedding plans. Nevertheless, she politely admires several caves, and as they walk along, to make conversation, she questions Aziz about his marriage. ". . . do come and see my wife," he tells her, feeling it is "more artistic to have his wife alive for a moment." And Adela blunderingly asks "Have you one wife or more than one?" Aziz-who is an enlightened, modern man and would never think of having more than one wife-is shocked. ". . . To ask an educated Indian Moslem how many wives he has-appalling, hideous!" He plunges into a cave "to recover his balance," while Adela, quite ignorant of her mistake, casually enters another.

Comment

Adela's blunder is typically British and patronizing; it illuminates once more the cause of the gulf of prejudice which separates the English and the Indians: ignorance, no more and no less. Furthermore, the conversation which Adela and Aziz have as they climb toward the highest cave focuses Adela's mind on love and marriage and helps to precipitate the coming crisis.

CHAPTER SIXTEEN

After a minute in the cave to restore his calm, Aziz goes out to look for Adela. When he can't find her, he becomes panicky, thinking she is lost. The guide is no help, and he strikes the man in the face for a punishment. Then suddenly he catches sight of Miss Quested on the road below. She seems to have come across a friend, for there is another lady, in a motor car, with her, and after a minute the two drive off together. Reassured, Aziz returns to the rock where he had left Mrs. Moore and is overjoyed to find Fielding there also. The Englishman explains that Miss Derek had run him up in her Maharani's auto after he missed the train. Then he inquires about Adela, and is shocked at the rude way in which the girl has run off. A servant comes to inform them that she has returned to Chandrapore with Miss Derek, and Fielding can hardly believe it. But to Aziz, of course, such impulsiveness seems the most natural thing in the world.

After Fielding has been taken to see one cave (it doesn't impress him), the three prepare to leave for Chandrapore themselves. But first Aziz must reassure Fielding that Adela is all right, for the Englishman senses that something is wrong and fears that she may have been ill or-he doesn't know what. Aziz doesn't share his fears, however, and after some jovial talk about the high cost of the picnic, they catch their train and sleep all the way home. When they arrive, however, the door of their carriage is rudely flung open by Mr. Haq, the Inspector of Police, who shocks them by saying in "shrill tones: 'Dr. Aziz, it is my highly painful duty to arrest you.'" Fielding thinks there must be some mistake, and Aziz, sobbing at the disgrace, tries to escape, but Fielding promises that whatever happens, he will see him through. They emerge into a chaotic scene at the station, with police and porters milling about everywhere, and before they can pass through it Fielding is called away by Mr. Turton. Aziz goes to prison alone.

Comment

The charge against Aziz is still a mystery, but we sense at once that his "crime" must somehow be related to the caves, and to Adela's mysterious departure with Miss Derek. Perhaps Mrs. Moore's uncanny second sight had operated again when she irrationally felt there was something evil in the cave she visited.

CHAPTER SEVENTEEN

When Fielding reaches Turton's side at the railway station, the Collector explains, almost speechless with rage, that "The worst thing in my whole career has happened . . . Miss Quested has been insulted in one of the Marabar caves." Fielding, sick, cannot believe it. Aziz is being accused of having assaulted Adela Quested! "She's mad," he exclaims, without thinking, and Turton, in a fury, insists that he "withdraw" that remark instantly. Fielding withdraws it "unconditionally . . . for the man half was mad himself."

Turton, trembling, goes on to say that all this trouble comes of consorting with the natives. It is obvious that he at least partially blames Fielding and his "modern ideas" for the tragedy, but he also feels that he himself is responsible. Fielding sees that the man's words are "dignified and pathetic" but thinks that they have nothing to do with Aziz. Whereas Turton has "decided to avenge the girl, he hope(s) to save the man."

Turton invites Fielding to an informal meeting at the Club that night, and Fielding agrees to come. Miss Quested is ill and cannot be seen, but Fielding is anxious to get more information. He senses that all the British in Chandrapore are abandoning reason and rallying to "the banner of race," but he hopes that he himself may preserve the logic of facts "though the herd has decided on emotion."

On his way out of the station, Turton stops some looting of Aziz's things which is going on among the natives, but he also glares with pure hostility at the Indians, thinking "I know what you're like at last; you shall pay for this, you shall squeal."

Comment

At last the hatred between the Indians and the English is really out in the open. The two seem to be facing each other across an unbridgeable gulf as they totter on the brink of a race war, and only the cosmopolitan and rational Fielding doesn't feel the need to align himself with his own people. It is ironic that Adela Quested, with her naive desire to get to know the natives, should have started all this - and it is probably inevitable that the critical event should have taken place in one of the terrifying Marabar caves.

CHAPTER EIGHTEEN

In this chapter Fielding goes to see McBryde, the Superintendent of Police and the "most reflective and best educated of Chandrapore officials." Despite his intelligence and air of courtesy, however, the Superintendent is hopelessly prejudiced against natives, believing that they are all "criminals at heart" because of the hot climate. He politely tells Fielding all he knows about the case - "That he (Aziz) followed her into the cave and made insulting advances. She hit him with her fieldglasses; he pulled at them and the strap broke, and that is how she got away." When Fielding expresses doubt about Aziz's guilt, however, McBryde becomes more hostile. He produces letters from Aziz's pocket, to show that the young man was arranging to "see women at Calcutta" and refuses to allow his fellow Englishman to see the prisoner at all. "Why mix yourself up with pitch?" he inquires. "Innocence or guilt, why mix yourself up?" Fielding is furious at this, and at the suggestion that "We shall all have to hang together, old man . . . you don't happen to know this poisonous country as well as I do, and you must take it from me that the general situation is going to be nasty at Chandrapore during the next few weeks. . . ." Fielding knows things will be "nasty," but he believes that a miscarriage of justice would be the nastiest thing of all. He winces when Aziz's treasured picture of his dead wife is brought in as further evidence of the young man's interest in women. But "wife indeed," thinks Mr. McBryde, whose face has become "inquisitive and slightly bestial," "I know these wives!"

Comment

Not only have the British hysterically rallied into a "herd," drawn by the banner of racial pride, but they are also, ironically, abandoning the very principles of honor and justice which made them feel so superior to the Indians in the first place. Earlier, we must remember, Ronny Heaslop had told his mother that he was not out here to behave "pleasantly" to the natives, but rather to "do justice and keep the peace." Now however, the British are abandoning the ideal of justice as easily as they dismissed the idea of "pleasantness." Only Fielding, who is, ironically, to be ostracized by his colleagues as a kind of traitor to the British cause and not a "sahib," stands firmly for the "British" ideals of justice and integrity.

CHAPTER NINETEEN

Going wholeheartedly over to the "Indian side," Fielding confers with Aziz's friend Hamidullah about a lawyer for the young man. Hamidullah, "the leading barrister of Chandrapore, with the dignified manner and Cambridge degree, [has] been rattled." He keeps worrying about the most politic way of approaching the English, and "at the moment when he was throwing in his lot with the Indians, [Fielding] realized the profundity of the gulf that divided him from them. They always do something disappointing . . . Aziz had tried to run away from the police . . . and now Hamidullah-instead of raging and denouncing, he temporized."

Hamidullah finally insists on calling in an Hindu lawyer so that the defense will "make a wider appeal." The man he chooses is "Amritrao, a Calcutta barrister, who [has] a high reputation professionally and personally, but who [is] notoriously anti-British."

After he returns to the school, Fielding has a curious conversation with Professor Godbole, who is on the verge of leaving for a new position in central India. He annoys Fielding by talking of trivial matters, but when the Englishman forces him to discuss the Aziz affair, he enigmatically replies that whatever happened in the cave was done by everyone. "When evil occurs, it expresses the whole of the universe," he says, and he goes on to explain that good and evil "are both of them aspects of my Lord. He is present in the one, absent in the other . . . yet absence implies presence, absence is non-existence, and we are therefore entitled to repeat 'Come, come, come, come.'"

Later that afternoon, Fielding goes to see Aziz, who is, however, "unapproachable through misery."

Comment

Indians, like Hamidullah, are "disappointing" in an emergency for the very reason that they are a subject people whose lives and careers depend solely on British whim. Naturally Aziz tried to escape and Hamidullah worries about policy; they know their British masters better than those masters know themselves, and they realize that the ideal of justice is only skin-deep.

Fielding's conversation with Professor Godhole reminds us that the incident in the Marabar caves has **metaphysical** as well as social overtones. Mrs. Moore, of course, had seen the caves at once in a kind of cosmic context, but with all the political flurry there has been since the arrest of Aziz, we need Professor Godbole's religious speculations to show us again that morality exists in a larger framework.

CHAPTER TWENTY

The British gather at their club that evening in a kind of exaltation, to defend Miss Quested's honor. Though Adela had not been especially popular with them, she is now the heroine of the hour. Mrs. Turton, who had pronounced her "not pukka," now calls her "my own darling girl."

Outside the club the Indians are beating drums as part of the Moslem festival of Mohurram, which is rapidly approaching, but naturally the noise adds to the feeling of apprehension, of "the natives are restless tonight," which grips the whole company. The men send their wives out of the room in order to discuss matters; panicky, they plan to send the women and children to the hills at once. Major Callendar arrives to report on Miss Quested's condition - she is better - and begins slyly to insult Fielding, who has been sitting quietly by. He knows the educator sympathizes with Aziz and blames the whole incident on him anyway, because he'd missed the train to the caves. Fielding controls himself with a great effort; he doesn't want to make a scene.

A few moments later, however, Ronny Heaslop-the fiancé of the "victim" -enters the room, and all the British, as a gesture of sympathy and solidarity, stand in his honor. All, that is, except Fielding. When Turton, annoyed, asks Fielding why he has remained seated, the schoolmaster replies that it is because "I believe Aziz to be innocent," and after a few more angry words from the Collector, he resigns from the Club. If Aziz is guilty, furthermore, he promises to resign from his service and leave India entirely.

Comment

In resigning from the Club, Fielding has taken the final step and severed all his significant social connections with the British colony. Some members actually respect him for his frankness, but to most he has simply proven once and for all that he is "not a sahib."

CHAPTER TWENTY-ONE

"Dismissing his regrets," Fielding leaves the Club, glad that he won't have the opportunity to pick up scraps of gossip there which he might report to his Indian friends later. He spends the evening with the Nawab Bahadur, Hamidullah, Mahmoud Ali and Aziz's other friends, planning the defense.

Comment

Fielding's integrity is thoroughly consistent and all-pervasive. Just as he declines to accept a double-standard of justice for Indians and English, he also refuses to use the kind of tactics against the British which they themselves are willing to use against the Indians.

CHAPTER TWENTY-TWO

In the meantime, Adela has been staying for several days with the McBrydes. "She had been touched by the sun, also hundreds of cactus spines had to be picked out of her flesh." In an important passage, Forster describes how Miss Derek and Mrs. McBryde examine her through a magnifying glass, picking out the tiny spines, which process develops "the shock that had begun in the cave ... People seemed very much alike, except that some would come close while others kept away." Like that of Mrs. Moore, Adela's experience in the Marabar caves leaves her revolted by her fellow man. All through her illness, she wants nothing more than to see Mrs. Moore, however. Not realizing that her companion has been as deeply affected as she has, she hopes that Mrs. Moore can drive away the "evil" that has been let "loose."

When Adela's temperature has dropped, Ronny comes to take her home. He tells her about the "Mohurram troubles" (rioting in the city) and about Aziz's forthcoming trial, in which she will have to appear and be cross-examined. When she asks about Mrs. Moore, he is strangely circumspect, explaining that Adela is likely to find his mother rather changed and "irritable."

Back at the bungalow, Adela finds that this is indeed so. She keeps wanting reassurance from Mrs. Moore - that she is doing the right thing, that the older woman sympathizes, etc. - yet she seems unable to get any response. "Mrs. Moore showed no inclination to be helpful. A sort of resentment emanated from her. She seemed to say: 'Am I to be bothered forever?'

Her Christian tenderness had gone, or had developed into a hardness, a just irritation against the human race; she had taken no interest at the arrest, asked scarcely any question . . ." Talking about the caves, Adela mentions the echo. "I can't get rid of it," she explains. "I don't suppose you ever will," Mrs. Moore replies rather unkindly - but then Mrs. Moore is suffering herself, though her son Ronny does not understand this. He is simply annoyed with her and reflects that she is "by no means the dear old lady outsiders supposed. India had brought her out into the open." Now she wants only to return to England, and Ronny is inclined to let her go, despite the heat.

Later that night, Adela tells Ronny - strangely - that Aziz is "innocent, I made an awful mistake." Immediately on saying this, she exclaims that her echo is better and adds that "Aziz is good. You heard your mother say so." Ronny tells her that his mother said nothing, but Adela seems to be suffering from the extraordinary hallucination that Mrs. Moore said "Dr. Aziz never did it." Worse yet, when Ronny, "to clear the confusion up," asks his mother about it, she denies having said anything, but then adds that "of course, he is innocent." Adela is terribly upset by this, and when Ronny tells her that now "the case has to come before a magistrate" because "the machinery has started," she is in tears. Ronny, furious with his mother, decides that she ought to leave India at once.

Comment

Both Adela and Mrs. Moore have had the same devastating experience in the caves, an experience of cosmic "panic and emptiness" which has led them-each in her own way-to abandon all faith in human values. Mrs. Moore, the same Mrs. Moore who told Ronny that "God is love," now rejects "all this rubbish about love," and though she knows Aziz is innocent, refuses to be bothered about his defense. Her state of revulsion with the world seems to be a stage in the mystical experience, which might eventually develop beyond negation to something else, though Forster has not suggested what.

When Adela, however, thinks she hears Mrs. Moore saying that Aziz is innocent, her "echo" seems to go away for a moment- as though the goblins of nihilism could be dispelled by human faith and trust. The question now is, can they be dispelled by anything, for any length of time?

CHAPTER TWENTY-THREE

This brilliant chapter describes Mrs. Moore's departure from India. No passage can be obtained so late in the year, so Mrs. Turton is prevailed upon to appeal to Lady Mellanby, the Lieutenant-Governor's wife, and this kind lady generously provides space for Mrs. Moore in her own cabin, since no other is available. Journeying across India, Mrs. Moore speculates about the cave and her experience in it. She had come to India wanting "to be one with the universe," a noble cosmos as she then envisioned it, a great backdrop for love and heroism. But "what had spoken to her in that scouredout cavity of granite? . . . Something very old and very small. Before time, it was before space also. Something snub-nosed, incapable of generosity- the undying worm itself," which mocks human existence and human values. From the train, Mrs. Moore can see a fortress called Asirgarh, which has "huge and noble bastions." As she passes it, she recognizes at last that there is something more than the Marabar worm in this world. And as her boat sails out of the harbor, she can see thousands of coconut palms rising above Bombay. "'So you thought an echo was India, you took the Marabar caves as final?" they laughed. 'What have we in common with them, or they with Asirgarh?'"

Comment

As she leaves India, Mrs. Moore, who had sunk to the nadir of despair in the days following her vision in the caves, seems to be coming out of her depression a little. If we take India as a kind of generalized symbol of the ultimate reality that underlies all civilizations-a placed closer to the paradoxical truths of the earth than any western land-Mrs. Moore seems to be recognizing at this point that reality is elusive, inexplicable, indescribable-that things are neither all-good nor all-bad, but only there, to be seen, passed, and remembered, like the caves, Bombay, and Asirgarh.

CHAPTER TWENTY-FOUR

The terrible Indian heat "accelerated its advance after Mrs. Moore's departure until existence had to be endured and crime punished with the thermometer at one hundred and twelve." In preparation for the trial, Adela has returned to Christianity, kneeling in prayer every morning. On the fateful day, she tries to pray, drinks a little brandy and leaves for court with the solicitous Turtons. "My echo has come back again, badly," she tells them-which is significant in view of what she is about to do.

At court, the British - most of the important members of the colony have turned up to offer Adela moral support - are placed in Ronny's private office, where they abuse the turncoat Fielding "vigorously" and rally round Adela with enthusiasm. The trial, from which Ronny is disqualified as magistrate by his relationship with Adela, is to be handled by his chief assistant, Mr. Das. Ronny thinks this is good: "Conviction was inevitable, so better let an Indian pronounce it, there would be less fuss in the long run." But many of the other British are outraged that an Indian should pronounce a verdict on a case involving an Englishwoman.

It is very hot in the courtroom and a beautiful, half-naked outcaste keeps the punkah (fan) going constantly. The trial begins with Mr. McBryde testifying that "the darker races are physically attracted by the fairer, but not vice versa," to which an unidentified Indian voice replies, "Even when the lady is so uglier than the gentleman?" Adela feels faint at the insult, and a seat is provided for her and her party on the platform. The Indians quickly object to all the British sitting above them, however, and so the whole group (including Adela) eventually climbs down. Adela feels better, though, now that she has seen all the people in the room, and thinks she will come through "all right."

The prosecution begins calling its witnesses and tries to prove that the crime was premeditated, that, for instance, Aziz tried to "get rid" of Mrs. Moore by "crushing her into a cave among his servants." The mention of Mrs. Moore provokes a great outcry from the Indians, however, who have heard that Mrs. Moore thought Aziz was innocent, and in the hullaballoo which ensues the old woman's name is Indianized into "Esmiss Esmoor, a Hindu goddess" - that is, she is, as it were, canonized in the native religion, which Ronny naturally finds "revolting." The crowd outside takes up the chant of "Esmiss Esmoor" with enthusiasm, then suddenly it stops, "as if the prayer had been heard."

Soon Adela is called to testify, and as she stands in the witness box "a new and unknown sensation protected her, like magnificent armor." "Across a sort of darkness," she tells her memories of the expedition, which now suddenly seems splendid and significant, to Mr. McBryde. When they get to the crucial moment, however, the moment of the assault in the cave, she stops short, asking for a chance to think. Then, astonishingly, as if out of nowhere, she denies that Aziz followed her into the cave. Fielding, in the audience, sees that she is "about to have a nervous breakdown and that his friend [has been] saved." And indeed, Adela confesses that "I'm afraid I have made a mistake," which of course leads Mr. Das to stop the trial at once, declaring that "the prisoner is released without one stain on his honor." The English, furious, leave in a white-faced group, while the Indians, for their part, immediately begin a wild celebration.

Comment

Adela's sensational confession is the **climax** of the long, dramatic Marabar caves story which is the central incident of the book, the heart of the plot. And perhaps it was the Hindu prayer to "Esmiss Esmoor" which suddenly helped the girl to grope her way out of the delusive Marabar darkness that had closed around her, into the simpler light of truth and faith. For the British, however, as we shall see, Adela's confession constitutes a social betrayal as grave as Fielding's defense of Aziz; many of them will always believe the Indian guilty, no matter what facts or logic are assembled in his behalf.

CHAPTER TWENTY-FIVE

By exonerating Aziz, Adela has "renounced her own people," and she finds herself being borne off by a mass of Indians. She hardly knows what she is doing and where she is going, so that when she collides with Fielding it is only natural that the gentlemanly Englishman should offer her his carriage. He promises Aziz that he will return to join in his celebration, but meanwhile he and Adela are carried away by his students, who heap the pair with garlands and pull their carriage through the bazaar. Finally they take refuge in Fielding's school, which is deserted for the moment, but Fielding wishes he could join in Aziz's victory party.

At the same time, Aziz and his friends are being borne in procession through the town, and the celebration shows signs of turning into a riot. There are rumours that the Nawab Bahadur's grandson, Nureddin, is being tortured at the hospital, so the mob rushes there, only to find that he is all right. Finally the Nawab Bahadur invites everyone to special "rejoicings" at his country home in Dilkusha, and the tension subsides, "for the heat was claiming its own. Unable to madden, it stupefied, and before long most of the Chandrapore combatants were asleep."

Comment

Fielding's ambiguous "bridge" - like position is emphasized by his sense of responsibility to Miss Quested, one of "his own" people, whom he feels he must rescue before he can join in Aziz's victory celebration. As we shall see, he will soon be increasingly torn by his loyalty to both combatants.

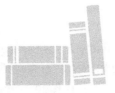

A PASSAGE TO INDIA

. . . .

CHAPTER TWENTY-SIX

Adela stays at Fielding's College for a time, during which they have a number of "curious conversations." At first, he is rather "curt" with her, wondering "Why make such a charge if you were going to withdraw it?" but he is soon convinced of the girl's sincerity, and finally comes to agree with her belief that she must have been ill, "hallucinated" by her experience in the cave. His sympathy for her is increased by his memory of Aziz's description of her as a "hag"; he doesn't feel that her looks should have anything to do with the case at issue.

Hamidullah comes by in the course of their first conversation after the trial, and Adela tries to explain her conduct to him, but he is bitter and resentful. He obviously wants Fielding to get rid of Adela as soon as possible, and to come out with him to the Nawab Bahadur's at once. But Fielding cannot cast off what he now believes to be a responsibility so easily. There is some question about where the girl is to stay, and he offers her his College as a temporary refuge, since he is about to leave with Hamidullah. She is on the verge of refusing when Ronny Heaslop comes to tell her that of course she can no longer stay with the Turtons, and that his own "bachelor" quarters would be unsuitable, so it is finally decided that Adela will stay on at Fielding's.

Ronny also brings the news that his mother, Mrs. Moore, has died on board the ship to England. Fielding and Adela are shocked and upset. "She was dead when they called her name this morning," Adela exclaims. But Hamidullah and Fielding agree that Ronny is entirely to blame. "An Indian May is no month to allow an old lady to travel in."

Later, when Fielding and the Indians are on their way to the Nawab Bahadur's, Hamidullah asks Amritrao "What sum Miss Quested ought to pay as compensation?" The answer, "Twenty thousand rupees," horrifies Fielding. "He couldn't bear to think of the queer honest girl losing her money and possibly her young man too. She advanced into his consciousness suddenly."

Comment

It almost seems as though Fielding has come to play the role which Mrs. Moore abandoned after her experience in the cave-the role of a living bridge between isolated men-for only he, now, is capable of sympathizing with both Adela and Aziz. He lacks Mrs. Moore's visionary, almost supernatural insight into events, however, and therefore runs no risk of becoming a saint (like "Esmiss Esmoor") in either the western or the Hindu firmament.

CHAPTER TWENTY-SEVEN

After the Victory Banquet, Aziz and Fielding lie on the roof of the Nawab Bahadur's house talking things over in the relatively cool night air. Aziz has been convinced by his Indian friends that he ought to seek a large sum in compensation from Miss Quested, and Fielding is trying to dissuade him. "You think that by letting Miss Quested off easily I shall make a better reputation for myself and Indians generally," Aziz says. "No, no. It will be put down to weakness and the attempt to gain promotion officially." In fact, he adds, he is determined to leave British India and get a job in a native state.

Fielding tries to explain to Aziz what a brave gesture Adela had made in the courtroom - "All her friends around her, the entire British Raj pushing her forward, she stops, sends the whole thing to smithereens" - but Aziz is unreceptive. Finally he tells Fielding he will "consult Mrs. Moore," for the news of the old English-woman's death has not yet been generally revealed. After he has talked about Mrs. Moore and her children a little more, Fielding cannot bear it and blurts out "I'm sorry to say Mrs. Moore's dead." But Hamidullah, who doesn't want the festive evening spoilt, tells Aziz that "he is trying to pull your leg," and Aziz believes him. Fielding, knowing that everyone will hear the truth in the morning, says no more. Indeed, as he lies in the dark, thinking of death, it occurs to him that "he had tried to kill Mrs. Moore this evening ... but she still eluded him and the atmosphere remained tranquil."

Comment

Mrs. Moore has become, like Mrs. Wilcox in *Howards End*, a spirit which broods over the story, giving to later events-as we shall see-a meaning and a structure they would not otherwise have.

CHAPTER TWENTY-EIGHT

Further details of Mrs. Moore's death and of the reaction to it are given in this chapter. The old lady was taken ill almost as soon as she came aboard ship, which Lady Mellanby found "needlessly distressing." In Chandrapore "a legend sprang up that an Englishman had killed his mother for trying to save an Indian's life - and there was just enough truth in this to cause annoyance to the authorities." Too, there are "signs of the beginning of a cult - earthenware saucers and so on," but "after a week or so, the rash died down."

Ronny tries to clear his conscience of guilt by telling himself "that his mother had left India at her own wish" and that in any case she had been "tiresome with her patronage of Aziz" and "a bad influence on Adela." His religion is "of the sterilized Public School brand, which never goes bad, even in the tropics," and he dutifully plans to put up a tablet to her in Northamptonshire.

As for Adela, Ronny feels that she is "unsuitable and humiliating," and he cannot possibly marry her - "it would mean the end of his career."

Comment

This is a final devastating picture of Ronny, the essence of the "pukka sahib" - smug, self-righteous and priggish. Unlike Fielding, he takes no responsibility for anything - especially not his mother's death or Adela's welfare, and unlike his mother, he is totally insensitive to any ideas but the socially acceptable, "sterilized" ones which he has made his own. More than anything else, he reminds us of Henry Wilcox in *Howards End*-indeed, of all the Wilcoxes except Ruth Wilcox - the practical men, the empire-builders, at the heart of whose "outer life of telegrams and anger" there is nothing but hypocrisy and a core of "panic and emptiness."

CHAPTER TWENTY-NINE

The "decomposition," as Forster calls it, of the Marabar affair goes on briskly. The Lieutenant-Governor visits Chandrapore and criticizes the intolerant behavior of the British. "Exempted by a long career in the secretariat from personal contact with the peoples of India," he is "able to deplore racial prejudice." In the meantime, Fielding is staying with Hamidullah, and Miss Quested remains at Fielding's college, since the school is closed for the moment. The Englishman finds himself increasingly sympathetic to the girl, who is universally ostracized by both Indians and English. Her "humility" is "touching," he thinks. "She never repined at getting the worst of both worlds; she regarded it as due punishment of her stupidity." He suggests that she write a letter of apology to Aziz, and she immediately does so, admitting, however, that she doesn't really like Indians after all.

Fielding's Indian friends are "a bit above themselves." Fielding continues to pressure Aziz to forego a large compensation from Adela. When he finally appeals to the memory of Mrs. Moore, the young doctor, who had been deeply stricken by her death, yields suddenly to his demands. As he had predicted, though, his fine gesture wins him "no credit with the English, who will go on believing him guilty to the end of their careers."

At last Ronny, who has been half-heartedly seeing her, breaks off his engagement to Adela, which the girl agrees is "far wiser of him." She plans to return to England, where she has "heaps of friends" of her own type, but of course, she tells Fielding, she regrets "the trouble I've brought on everyone here ... I can never get over it." She and Fielding, in their last talk, decide that "love" is impossible - and as for the experience in the cave, they conclude "indifferently" that the culprit must have been the guide. Neither, however, can quite forget Mrs. Moore's strange knowledge of Aziz's innocence. Was it "telepathy?" they wonder. "A friendliness, as of dwarfs shaking hands, was in the air. Both man and woman were at the height of their powers-sensible, honest, even subtle . . . yet they were dissatisfied."

Adela returns to England. She is in a daze until she reaches Egypt, where "the atmosphere altered. The clean sands heaped on each side of the canal seemed to wipe off everything that was difficult and equivocal . . ." Suddenly she realizes that "her first duty" in England will be to look up Mrs. Moore's other two children, Ralph and Stella.

Comment

Honest and sensitive as Adela and Fielding are, they cannot make real contact with each other. Beneath the vast mysterious sky of India, they are "dwarfs shaking hands." Both see that the visionary insight of a Mrs. Moore is even more necessary to meaningful relationships than the liberal good-will of people like themselves. Perhaps this is why Adela suddenly feels so strongly that she must find Mrs. Moore's other children-for though things seem to resolve themselves into a more comprehensible western order and clarity in Egypt, she knows that the "muddle" and "mystery" of India is the underlying truth of the universe.

CHAPTER THIRTY

Another result of the trial is a temporary peace between the Hindus and Moslems of Chandrapore, who are usually feuding. Mr. Das, the presiding Magistrate and a Hindu, even asks Aziz, who fancies himself a poet, to contribute some verses to a new magazine, edited by his brother-in-law. Trying to write something which will appeal to all, Aziz begins to feel the stirrings of a kind of patriotism, a love for the "vague and bulky figure of a mother-land." He decides definitely to leave British India and to take service in a native state, though his friend Hamidullah reminds him that he can hardly afford to lose his British salary, which is higher than anything "those savage Rajahs" will pay. Hamidullah reproaches him for having allowed Miss Quested to get off without paying a large compensation; if she had, Aziz would be independent now. Then Hamidullah adds news of a "naughty rumour" that has been going about lately. "When Miss Quested stopped in the College, Fielding used to visit her . . . rather too late in the evening, the servants say." Aziz tries to laugh at this, but he is obviously upset by it.

Comment

The seeds of suspicion have been sown between Aziz and Fielding, and they will slowly ripen into the hostility on Aziz's part which motivates the final action of the book.

CHAPTER THIRTY-ONE

Aziz, who lacks a "sense of evidence," soon persuades himself that the rumours about Fielding and Miss Quested are true. When he confronts Fielding with the story, however, his friend becomes annoyed. "You little rotter!" he exclaims, disgusted with Aziz for taking such obviously foolish gossip seriously. The Indian is "cut to the heart," both by Fielding's phrase and by the mistake that he himself has made. Over dinner the two try to make it up, but there is a good deal of constraint between them now, and their friendship seems more difficult to maintain than ever-especially because Fielding, under orders from the Lieutenant-Governor, has resumed his membership in the British Club. He tells Aziz that he expects to go to England for a short vacation quite soon, as his service is "anxious to get me away from Chandrapore for a bit. It is obliged to value me highly, but does not care for me."

Aziz, of course, assumes that Fielding will resume his relationship with Miss Quested in England, and, indeed, by the time Fielding leaves, their friendship has deteriorated to a point where the suspicious and impulsive Indian, quick to jump to conclusions, is convinced that Fielding has gone to England to marry Adela and get hold of the money which he, Aziz, had so generously relinquished. "'Where are my twenty thousand rupees?' he thought. He was absolutely indifferent to money . . . yet these rupees haunted his mind, because he had been tricked about them, and allowed them to escape overseas, like so much of the wealth of India."

Comment

At last India-the heat, the confusion, the suspicion, the horrible, panicky boum of the Marabar caves-has succeeded in coming between the only two in the book, Aziz and Fielding, who seemed to be effectively building a bridge between East and West. Of course, Aziz's own personality is at the root of the trouble, for if he weren't so ready to believe the worst of his friend, things would be all right. But Aziz's original naive and warm-hearted trust and friendliness were corrupted into this suspicious coldness by the treatment which he received from the British, so that ultimately both sides, East and West, are responsible for the situation.

CHAPTER THIRTY-TWO

As he journeys westward, away from India, Fielding finds himself increasingly relieved and refreshed by the orderly western landscape, and by the western sense of form, so different from the intricate muddle of India. Venice, especially, seems to him to embody "the harmony between the works of man and the earth that upholds them, the civilization that has escaped muddle, the spirit in a reasonable form, with flesh and blood subsisting." And as for the Mediterranean, "the Mediterranean is the human norm," home of the rational spirit rationally perceiving a coherently organized universe.

Comment

The difference between India and the West, as Forster outlines it in this chapter, seems to be the difference between a humanistic (man-centered) world-view (in the West) and a more mystical cosmic view of things (in India), in which man and his works count for as little (or as much) as any other phenomena. Forster has said that he took the title of *A Passage to India* from Walt Whitman's poem, "Passage to India," a poem in which the soul's passage to India is a mystical experience, a journey into contact with the cosmos. But if, then, the passage to India is such a mystical journey, Fielding's passage away from India is a voyage home to "the human norm," the everyday rational spirit which confronts and controls ordinary facts and does not seek for any meaning beyond the normal order.

CHAPTER THIRTY-THREE

Chapter thirty-three begins the third section of *A Passage to India*, the section called Temple, which Forster himself described as a "coda" to the main action of the novel. Two years have passed and Professor Godbole, now an important official in a native state, is participating in a major Hindu festival, a ceremony (rather like the western Christmas) which commemorates the birth of the god Krishna as a man in the world of men. As he intones a hymn in the midst of the typically Indian muddle around the altar (on which God is love [sic] has been inscribed in English by an uneducated Indian draftsman), Professor Godbole finds himself remembering "an old woman he had met in Chandrapore days." In his religious trance he feels he loves her - and equally he loves, or tries to love, a wasp he had seen somewhere, perhaps on a stone.

After some more singing, the "Birth" of the god takes place. The Rajah-ruler of the native state-is carried in on a litter to participate in the ceremony. He is a gravely ill man, and we learn that his Moslem physician, Dr. Aziz, is waiting for him in another part of the palace.

After the central rituals of the "Birth" are performed by the Rajah, Professor Godbole and the other priests, the people celebrate with games and dances. Throughout, Professor Godbole finds that he cannot shake off the thought of the old Englishwoman - Mrs. Moore - and the wasp. It pleases him, finally, that he has at least this small capacity for the impersonal religious love Hinduism preaches. "One old Englishwoman and one little, little wasp," he thinks. "It does not seem much, still it is more than I am myself."

Comment

In his valuable little book on Forster, Lionel Trilling asks, perhaps rhetorically: "Why so many Moslems and so few Hindus? Why so much Hindu religion and so little Moslem?" - an important and perceptive question. Probably the answer is that, in Forster's view, the Moslems are almost as alien in India as the British are, conveying as much of a sense of the strangeness of the land as the British do. The "real" India, if there is such a place, is for Forster, as it was for Walt Whitman, Hindu-for only the deliberately amorphous and mystical Hindu religion, with its innumerable lesser deities and its one all-pervading, indefinable, "philosophical" god, Brahm, seems to take into account all the mystery and muddle of the inexplicable cosmos that India symbolizes.

The wasp on which Professor Godbole meditates in this chapter, incidentally, appeared earlier in Mrs. Moore's thoughts - in chapter three - and its reappearance here, inexplicably associated with the Hindu's memories of the old woman, seems like another touch of the semi-supernatural, another indication of Mrs. Moore's spiritual power, persisting beyond the grave.

CHAPTER THIRTY-FOUR

As Dr. Aziz leaves the palace, he encounters "his old patron" Godbole (who helped him obtain his job with the Rajah), and Godbole abstractedly informs him that another old acquaintance, Fielding, is likely to have arrived at the European guest house on an official visit today. But Aziz, who is still convinced that his former friend treacherously married Adela Quested on reaching England, doesn't want to think about the Englishman.

Aziz has been content working with Godbole and his Rajah in the Hindu state of Mau, even though there are no other Moslems here to speak of. The trial left him permanently disillusioned with the English - even, because of his suspicions, with Fielding - and he has refused to open any of his friend's letters from England. Life passes "pleasantly" in Mau, however. He has his children with him and writes a good deal of poetry. The first real crisis in this comfortable new life has been arrival of Fielding. He finds a note at his house, containing routine inquiries about the place - "When would they pay their respects to His Highness? Was it correct that a torchlight procession would take place? If so, might they view it?" etc. - which he angrily tears up.

Comment

Earlier in this chapter, Forster comments on how things have changed in India, with the British no longer wielding the kind of absolute power that they had had a few years ago. Of course Aziz's trial and vindication did not primarily bring about this change, but Aziz himself, with his changed attitude, represents a country which will no longer stand for the kind of overbearing smugness and intolerance which had characterized the British Raj for so long. And the young doctor's court victory was no doubt a kind of minor herald of the larger Indian victory that Forster thinks may be soon to come.

CHAPTER THIRTY-FIVE

The morning after the "Birth" celebration, Aziz takes his children for a walk to a local shrine. Up at the hilltop holy place, they meet some prisoners, one of whom will be chosen by lot for release that night, in honor of the continuing Hindu festival. The prisoners inquire about the Raja's health, and Aziz tells them he is well, though he knows that the man is actually dead. "His death was being concealed lest the glory of the festival were dimmed."

As the children run about, they catch sight of two Englishmen climbing toward the shrine-Fielding and his brother-in-law! Suddenly the Englishmen are attacked by a swarm of bees, and the brother-in-law is stung. Aziz helps beat off the bees, and Fielding greets him coolly. But they've exchanged very few words when Aziz addresses Fielding's brother-in-law as "Mr. Quested," at which Fielding exclaims "Who on earth do you suppose I've married?" I'm only Ralph Moore," says the boy, blushing, and Fielding adds "Quested? Quested? Don't you know that my wife was Mrs. Moore's daughter?" Aziz is furious at himself and terribly upset. After some explanations from Fielding he leaves, crying "Please do not follow us, whomever you marry. I wish no Englishman or Englishwoman to be my friend." But "he returned to the house excited and happy. It had been an uneasy, uncanny moment when Mrs. Moore's name was mentioned, stirring memories. 'Esmiss Esmoor' ... - as though she was coming to help him."

Comment

Mrs. Moore's spirit, like Mrs. Wilcox's, is powerful even after her death. Just as Mrs. Wilcox had influenced the course of events through her relationship with Margaret, so Mrs. Moore-in the union of Fielding and her daughter Stella-lives on, at least partly to reconcile Aziz, the Indian who loved her, with Fielding, the Englishman he once had loved.

CHAPTER THIRTY-SIX

Despite the death of the Rajah, and though there are two claimants to the throne in the palace, the Hindu festival "flowed on, wild and sincere, and all men loved each other, and avoided by instinct whatever could cause inconvenience or pain." But Aziz, Forster tells us, "could not understand this, any more than an average Christian could. He was puzzled that Mau should suddenly be purged from suspicion and self-seeking."

Towards sunset he remembers that he had promised to bring a tin of ointment to the European Guest House for Ralph Moore's bee sting. On his way, he passes the Hindu religious procession, which is just starting out for the Mau tank (reservoir) where the final ceremony of the festival will take place. When he arrives at the Guest House, he finds no one there. Going from room to room, "inquisitive, malicious," he comes upon some letters, one from Heaslop to Fielding and one from Adela Quested to Stella Moore Fielding. He reads them with interest; they are "all so friendly and sensible, written in a spirit he could not command." Suddenly he is interrupted by the entrance of Ralph Moore, who has been resting in the next room.

Aziz rather coldly asks about the bee stings, and Ralph answers that "they throb, rather." After Dr. Aziz has examined him with scarcely concealed hostility, he openly challenges the Indian: "You should not treat us like this ... Dr. Aziz, we have done you no harm." "No, of course, your great friend Miss Quested did me no harm at the Marabar," Aziz replies bitterly. Outside they can hear the voices of the festival of love. "Mixed and confused in their passage, the rumours of salvation entered the Guest House." Aziz and Ralph move out onto the porch, where they talk more amicably. Aziz's heart is softened towards the strange young Englishman, and when he asks "Can you always tell whether a stranger is your friend?" and the other answers "Yes," he replies: "Then you are an Oriental," - the very words he had spoken to Mrs. Moore at that fateful first meeting in the mosque.

Aziz and Ralph decide to row out on the lake, where they can get a good view of the Hindu ceremony. Fielding and Stella are already there, watching from a boat. Crossing the water, Ralph Moore points out the tomb of the Rajah's father to Aziz. It contains an image of the king, "made to imitate life at enormous expense," which the Indian had never seen before, though he frequently rowed on the lake. He begins to feel that his companion is "not so much a visitor as a guide."

Near the other shore of the lake, Aziz and Ralph get a good view of the wild Hindu ceremony. The singers are "praising God without attributes," and preparing "to throw God away, God himself, (not that God can be thrown) into the storm. Thus was He thrown year after year . . . scapegoats, husks, emblems of passage; a passage not easy, not now, not here, not to be apprehended except when it is unattainable: the God to be thrown was an emblem of that." As they watch, the strangers lose track of where they are, and suddenly the two boats-Aziz's and Fielding's-collide, and all four are thrown into the water. At that very moment, the ceremony reaches its climax-guns are fired, drums beaten, and drowning all, there is an "immense peal of thunder . . . like a mallet on the dome." A moment later the rain pours down, settling in "steadily to its job of wetting everybody and everything through."

Comment

Even more than his sister Stella, Ralph Moore is the spiritual heir of Mrs. Moore. He speaks in the same gentle, nervously perceptive tones, has the same uncanny intuitions, and even evokes the same response from Aziz ("Then you are an Oriental"). Through him and his sister, a final if temporary reconciliation is brought about between Aziz and Fielding.

The scene on the lake is, in fact, a fitting symbol of that reconciliation. The Hindu festival is a feast of love, and of the god's incarnation as Man, rather like the Christian Christmas, in which the Birth of God as man brings about, at least temporarily, universal peace and good-will. When the two European boats collide, and their occupants are dumped into the water, the wetting they get is like a kind of baptism-total though temporary immersion in the waters of love, and the rain which immediately follows is like a kind of blessing from the heavens, for in hot climates such as India's the rains are always a sign of refreshment and renewal.

How can this triumphant renewal, this festival of love, be reconciled with Mrs. Moore's nihilistic vision at the caves, with Professor Godbole's passive acceptance of Krishna's absence, and with the horrible "panic and emptiness" of the caves themselves? K. W. Gransden, in his useful study of Forster, points out that in Hinduism-which, we have noted, is the religious expression of India, for Forster-Shiva, the destroyer, and Brahm or Krishna, the creator, are both aspects of the same divinity, co-existent forces in the same universe. What is destroyed, in Hinduism, must always be renewed, and thus, for Forster, the cosmos expresses itself, a cosmos in which life and death are equally inexplicable facts. ". . . Fragmentation, collapse, may destroy the one, but the fragments of that one can in some mystical way be reassembled," Gransden comments. "Mrs. Moore's collapse at the caves, her vision of the hollowness of things, was something she personally could not survive; yet her influence survives the collapse, her perception of the collapse does not exclude renewal: in Hinduism the creator and the destroyer are two aspects of the divine."

CHAPTER THIRTY-SEVEN

"Friends again, yet aware that they [can] meet no more, Aziz and Fielding [go] for their last ride in the Mau jungles." Though the Hindu festival and the death of the Rajah have conspired to keep Fielding from doing much business, thus making his visit officially a failure, on a personal level it has been a success: he and Aziz are thoroughly reconciled, and Aziz even produces a letter for Fielding to deliver to Adela Quested, thanking her for her courageous honesty two years before. "I want to do kind actions all round and wipe out the wretched business of the Marabar forever," he explains to Fielding.

As they ride along, they discuss Fielding's marriage, which is apparently "not quite happy" because his wife Stella, with whom he is passionately in love, has inherited some of her mother's mystical propensities. The two friends know that they will never meet again, because "socially they had no meeting-place" anymore, now that Fielding has "thrown in his lot with Anglo-India by marrying a countrywoman." But they are still fond of each other and want to settle things between them. Aziz finally proposes that when "the Turtons and the Burtons ... clear out" and India is an independent nation, he and Fielding can be friends again. In the meantime, he and his children must drive the British away. "Why can't we be friends now?" asks Fielding, holding him affectionately. "It's what I want. It's what you want."

"But the horses didn't want it-they swerved apart; the earth didn't want it, sending up rocks through which riders must pass single file; the temples, the tank, the jail, the palace, the birds, the carrion, the Guest House, that came into view as they issued from the gap and saw Mau beneath; they didn't want it, they said in their hundred voices,`No, not yet,' and the sky said, `No, not there.'"

Comment

The skillfully compressed and lyrical last paragraph of *A Passage to India*, quoted above, summarizes one of the chief **themes** of the novel-the isolation of man from man, which the book's central relationship, between an Indian and an Englishman, also symbolizes. When men can meet in perfect equality and freedom, Forster seems to be saying, then the "rainbow bridge" of friendship can be built. In other words, only when India is as independent as England will the representatives of the two nations, Fielding and Aziz, be able to relate fully and warmly to each other, all strangeness forgotten or ignored. Thus, to the motto of *Howards End* - "Only connect" - *A Passage to India* adds the knowledge that life's profoundest and most meaningful connections can only be made, if the heavens will them, between equals. And in the end it is significant that it is the will of things, not people, of the intractable Indian landscape, not the riders, that the friends be divided. As the book began, so it concludes, with the enormous, all-controlling Indian sky mysteriously influencing the destinies of men.

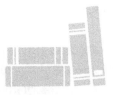

A PASSAGE TO INDIA

. . . .

Dr. Aziz

A young Moslem doctor, warm-hearted, inconsistent, impulsive, outgoing. He is a widower and the father of three children, writes poetry and is generally popular among Indians. His attempts to ingratiate himself with the few English whom he admires and who have been kind to him-namely, Fielding and Mrs. Moore-lead to nothing but the Marabar disaster, however, and he ends up being suspicious, patriotic and intensely anti-British, much of his warmly extroverted spirit killed by the trauma of his arrest and trial in Chandrapore.

An interesting question that might be raised in connection with Aziz is whether or not he could have even been capable of making any advances to Adela Quested in the Marabar Caves. Most readers and critics would assume, with Fielding, that Aziz was absolutely innocent-in thought as well as in deed. On the other hand, it could be pointed out that he had been thinking about women beforehand, as Mr. McBryde discovered, though, of course, his thoughts were entirely of "beautiful women" and he considers Adela emphatically plain. Still, might the Marabar have had as upsetting an effect on him as it did on Mrs. Moore and Adela? Could it have reversed all his usual values, causing only the "old and "snub-nosed" forces of the libido-uncontrollable passions without discrimination or discipline-to come to the surface? Despite the interesting speculations of certain critics, we must definitely dismiss this possibility, since we remain in Aziz's consciousness throughout the time of the cave **episode**. Nonetheless, the idea is relevant if only insofar as it sheds light both on Aziz's personality and on the mysteriously destructive influence of the caves.

Aziz, after all, though he is innocent in the incident with Adela Quested, is not wholly the simple and childishly friendly spirit he may at first seem to be. He has a very real streak of cruelty in him, as we can see in his treatment of Ralph Moore at the end of the book. And though this cruelty and vindictiveness may have been developed and intensified by his terrible experience with the British at Chandrapore, his earlier unpleasantness to Dr. Panna Lal shows that the seeds of it were always there. Like many impulsive, inconsistent people, Aziz is warm-hearted - but selfish; outgoing - but temperamental; quick to make friends - but equally adept at enmity.

Mrs. Moore

The elderly, "red-faced" and "white-haired" mother of Ronny Heaslop, the British City Magistrate in Chandrapore. At first gentle and loving - much like Mrs. Wilcox in *Howards End* - she, like Aziz, has suffered a radical personality change by the end of the book as a result of her experience in the Marabar. She becomes withdrawn and irritable, no longer caring at all for that "rubbish" about love in which she had believed at the beginning. Nevertheless, the Indians, who had been moved by her earlier friendliness, continue to sense her extraordinary spirit and her underlying faith in Aziz's innocence, and some of them even worship her as a kind of Hindu saint - "Esmiss Esmoor."

The crisis in Mrs. Moore's consciousness-her frightening experience in the caves-is in a sense the central **metaphysical** crisis of A Passage to India, and Mrs. Moore's mind is the vehicle for Forster's ideas. She had come to India ready to be "one with the universe." Contemplating a wasp (like Professor Godbole later), she murmured "Pretty dear," loving all things because of her underlying belief that "God . . . is . . . love," the tenderly "religious strain" in her which her son Ronny so vehemently distrusted. In the cave, however, she discovered that the universe, which she was so anxious to love and which she had hopefully thought so loving, also included "something very old and very small. Before time, it was before space also. Something snub nosed, incapable of generosity-the undying worm itself." And it is this discovery which so utterly dislocates Mrs. Moore's personality that, all tenderness gone, even for Aziz whom she had loved, she becomes overnight an irritable old woman, abstracted from reality, abandoning all thoughts of love and relationship.

Despite the change in her attitudes, however, Mrs. Moore retains her almost supernatural qualities: her perception, her aura of grace, her mystical understanding of events and people. As Adela lies in agony at the McBryde's bungalow, totally demolished by her experience in the caves, she longs only for Mrs. Moore, for she senses that Mrs. Moore, and Mrs. Moore only, somehow knows the truth. And, in the end, though she refuses to testify, Mrs. Moore does speak the truth, telling Adela - and, indirectly, all of India - that Aziz is innocent, and thereby dispelling the horrifying echo which has so haunted the sickened girl.

Finally, too, Mrs. Moore herself begins a slow wing back to a more balanced view of the universe, an upswing which, again, parallels the philosophical upswing of the book itself. As she travels past the magnificent fortress of Asirgarh, Mrs. Moore realizes that there is more to India - to the cosmos-than "the undying worm." Despite the worm, there is nobility, there is love. Perhaps God, then, is both love and death. This is what the novel, after all, with its final festival of love replacing the nihilism of the caves, seems to be saying. God, in Hinduism, the central philosophical pattern of *A Passage to India*, is both the destroyer and the creator of innumerable worlds.

Adela Quested

A "queer, honest girl," plain-flatchested, freckled - but intelligent. Her doubts about her forthcoming marriage, plus the frightening emptiness of the Marabar caves, lead her to make a feverish accusation against Aziz - indeed, it is the "snub-nosed" forces of her own libido, rather than of his, which are unleashed against her - but when she realizes she has probably suffered an hallucination, she bravely withdraws her charge in open court, despite the shock and disapproval of the entire British colony. Thus, in the end, she is in the unenviable position of being ostracized by everyone in Chandrapore - the Indians because of her charge against Aziz, and the British because of her failure to maintain their anti-Indian posture.

In a way, Adela, a kind of Bloomsbury intellectual who "means well," brings about the central trouble of *A Passage to India* by her bungling, "liberal" desire to "see India," just as the meddling, "liberal" interference of the Schlegels in Leonard

Bast's life causes the central crisis of *Howards End*. Bloomsbury ethics, if not thoroughly out, are not the last word in morality, Forster seems to be saying. At home, we are told, Adela has "heaps of friends" like herself - and no doubt the author would include Margaret and Helen Schlegel among them.

Ronny Heaslop

An unpleasant young man, Adela's fiancé, Mrs. Moore's son by an earlier marriage, and the British City Magistrate in Chandrapore. The Indians, to whom he had once been friendly, have come to dislike him; they call him "Red-Nose" in angry mockery. Arrogant, self-righteous, priggish and smug, he thinks he is doing the right thing in India ("doing justice and keeping the peace") but he has betrayed many of the ideals of thought and friendship to which he had at least lip service when a boy in England.

In many ways Ronny parallels the Wilcoxes of *Howards End* and perhaps indicates a clarifying of Forster's attitude toward such "business minds." In *Howards End* Forster had Margaret Schlegel say that "More and more do I refuse to draw my income and sneer at those who guarantee it." Though he depicted the Wilcoxes as arrogant, thick-skinned, smug, like Ronny and most of the other English in *A Passage to India* (except Fielding), he ended up by seeming at least qualifiedly to approve of them: they were the practical men who must unite with the intellectuals ("the prose with the passion") to build a better England. But in *A Passage to India* he seems to have withdrawn whatever approval he may ever have given. In the end, the English, like Ronny Heaslop, don't even adhere to their own proudly-expressed ideals of justice and integrity.

Fielding

A middle-aged, gentlemanly, intelligent Englishman, the Principal of the Local Government College in Chandrapore, "with a belief in education." Like Margaret in *Howards End*, Fielding tries to be a bridge between the divided social groups in the book-in this case, the English and the Indians. His friendship with Aziz is deep and warm, as is his loyalty to the Indian at the time of his trial. But their relationship cannot withstand the burden of suspicion and hostility which the British mistreatment of Aziz has laid upon it. In the end, too, though Fielding is as honorable, intelligent and affectionate as ever, his marriage to a countrywoman (Stella Moore) puts him irrevocably on the British side of things, and cuts him off forever from Indians like Aziz.

At least, however, Fielding has reached beyond the prison of his race and nationality to make a tentative connection with those who are different from himself, and for this he is certainly to be respected. Indeed, if there are any future "connections" to be made, Forster thinks, they will be made by thoughtful men like Fielding. Perhaps the only lack in him, finally, is that supernatural" quality (for want of a better word) which Mrs. Moore has, and which her children Ralph and Stella inherit from her, that quality of almost saintly perception which transcends normal intelligence and education like Fielding's. Thus Mrs. Moore can see at once the cosmic implications of the Marabar caves, while Fielding finds them merely ordinary. Thus Ralph Moore can guide Aziz across a lake on which Fielding would only flounder, without oars. Thus Stella's mystical leanings, so like her mother's "religious strain," are unintelligible to Fielding and threaten to drive a wedge between husband and wife. But still, despite this lack-or perhaps even because of it-Fielding is an example of what the ordinary, the natural man, as opposed to the extraordinary, supernormal seer, can accomplish in the way of "connection" and relationship" in daily life, without the aid of any religion but the humanistic religion of kindliness and tolerance.

Hamidullah And Mahmoud Ali

Aziz's friends, Moslems, British-educated, intelligent, witty Indians, both lawyers, who suffer as Aziz does from the British prejudice against Indians. Like Aziz, they are embittered by the Chandrapore trial and become, as result, even more nationalistic and anti-British than they were before.

Professor Godbole

A teacher of music at Fielding's college, a Hindu, whose absorption in philosophical speculations doesn't keep him from seeing through the texture of daily life to the cosmic and human realities beneath. In fact, his mystical acceptance of the universe becomes, at the end, a pattern which Forster seems to think all men would do well to follow.

Despite Forster's evident affection for him, however, Godbole is a mysterious figure throughout the book, and we are never quite sure how to take him. His song to Krishna expresses the nihilism of the universe, and his refusal to discuss the caves indicates also a Mrs. Moore-like perception of their secret. Unlike Mrs. Moore, though, he is apparently able to temper this perception with acceptance of things, an acceptance which is the **theme** of the last section of the book, Temple. Thus he is very like Mrs. Moore in providing a vehicle through which Forster can express his "Indian" metaphysic-the negation of the Krishna song and the positive acceptance of Temple, God the Destroyer and God the Creator. It is significant, after all, that Godbole is the only real Hindu in a book so full of Hindu philosophy. And what about the implications of his name, which in English means "trunk" or "stem" or swelling out" of God?

Ralph And Stella Moore

Mrs. Moore's children by a later marriage. Ralph, in particular, seems to be Mrs. Moore's "spiritual heir," a kind of reincarnation of his mother, with all her nervousness, gentleness, and uncanny insight into people and events. Aziz, at first bitterly hostile to him (in Temple) is soon won over by this startling resemblance of his to the beloved "Esmiss-Esmoor," and in the wild scene on the lake in the next-to-the-last chapter of *A Passage to India* Aziz is astonished by the strange, almost supernatural way in which Ralph guides him across the lake, straight to the legendary image of a Hindu king which he, Aziz, has never seen before, despite many trips in its vicinity.

Though we never actually meet her, we are told that Stella Moore, too-a beautiful girl who marries Cyril Fielding-has inherited many of her mother's mystical propensities, a fact which we learn has tended to cut her off from her husband, who does not share either her interests or her abilities. Nevertheless, we feel that in the end all will be well between Cyril and Stella; he, with his developed humanity, educated heart, and she, with her mystical, supernormal perceptiveness and love, will make it so.

Mr. And Mrs. Turton

The highest ranking British official in Chandrapore and his wife. Well-intentioned but smug, self-righteous and intolerant people, along the lines of Ronny Heaslop in this book and the Wilcoxes in *Howards End.*

Mr. McBryde

The British Superintendent of Police in Chandrapore-better educated and more thoughtful than most Englishmen in the town but with the same blind prejudice against "natives," who, he declares, are all made criminals at heart by the hot climate in which they live. (He never explains how he, who was born and raised in the same hot Indian climate, escaped the same criminal fate.)

Major Callendar

The Civil Surgeon, Aziz's superior at the hospital. An exceptionally intolerant and bad-tempered man who is forever making snide remarks against the Indians and against those Englishmen, like Fielding, who side with the Indians. Throughout the book he takes advantage of Aziz, exploiting his professional talents without making any effort to treat him decently in return.

The Nawab Bahadur

A rich local Moslem landowner, who owes his title to the British but who nevertheless maintains his spiritual independence and "Indianness." His strange superstitions and belief in the supernatural contrast vividly with the modern motorcar he keeps, his rational attitude toward the British and his general political sophistication and enlightenment.

Mr. Das

Ronny's conscientious Indian assistant and the presiding Magistrate at Aziz's trial. With a superhuman effort he manages to control the strife-torn courtroom, thereby proving that an Indian can administer justice as fairly and efficiently as an Englishman.

Miss Derek

A visiting Englishwoman who represents all that is most irresponsible and reprehensible about the British Raj in India. A companion to a Maharani in a Native State, she coolly takes her employer's car on her vacation without asking permission, because she cannot imagine that "natives" could have as good a use for the vehicle as she does.

HOWARDS END AND A PASSAGE TO INDIA

....

EARLY CRITICISM

Although *Howards End* and *A Passage to India* are generally accepted by critics as E. M. Forster's most successful and important novels, there has been a certain flurry of controversy over which work is better. Perhaps the best known opponents in this conflict have been F. R. Leavis, one of the most influential literary critics in England today, and Lionel Trilling, this counterpart on the American literary scene. Leavis asserted in 1938-in one of the earliest and shrewdest essays on Forster's work-that *Howards End*, while obviously the work of a mature and experienced novelist, "exhibits crudity of a kind to shock and distress the reader as Mr. Forster hasn't shocked or distressed him before."

LEAVIS

Leavis felt that, although the portraits of the Schlegels and Wilcoxes were reasonably accurate, Leonard Bast was an unreal creation, "a mere external grasping at something that lies outside the author's firsthand experience," and that, worse, the marriage between Margaret and Henry Wilcox was totally incredible. "Nothing in the exhibition of Margaret's or Henry Wilcox's character," he wrote, "makes the marriage credible or acceptable; even if we were to seize for motivation on the hint of a panicky flight from spinsterhood in the already old-maidish Margaret, it might go a little way to explain her marrying such a man, but it wouldn't in the least account for the view of the affair the novelist expects us to take" -that is, for its function as a kind of symbolic union of two major forces in English life, the practical and the intellectual. Leavis, like many other readers, cannot believe, in other words, that a sensitive, imaginative, cultivated woman like Margaret Schlegel could ever be attracted to an "obtuse, egotistic, unscrupulous, self-deceiving" businessman like Henry Wilcox. Furthermore, he felt that Forster was mistaken in his judgment of Margaret, and of intellectuals generally. "Intelligence and sensitiveness such as *Howards End* at its finest represents need not be so frustrated by innocence and inexperience as the unrealities of the book suggest."

TRILLING

Lionel Trilling, on the other hand, in a highly-regarded study of Forster which he produced in 1944, claimed that "*Howards End* is undoubtedly Forster's masterpiece; it develops to their full the **themes** and attitudes of the early books and throws back upon them a new and enhancing light. It justifies these attitudes by connecting them with a more mature sense of responsibility." Though he was in substantial agreement with Leavis about Henry Wilcox's character (he nowhere directly faced the question of the marriage, however), Trilling seemed to accept

Forster's description of the Margaret-Henry relationship more or less at face value. "Margaret's impulse toward Henry Wilcox is precisely the same as Helen's had been toward Paul," he noted, "except that hers is more explicit and less sexually romantic. Henry is one of the race that runs the world, and he is masculine. She cannot continue to despise the people who control the ships and trains that carry 'us literally people around.'" Elsewhere he explained that "*Howards End* is not only a novel of the class war but of the war between men and women. Margaret, like Helen, is to respond to the Wilcox masculinity . . . More perceptive than Helen, she knows this masculinity for what it is-far from adequate - but she accepts it more simply, demanding less of it." His reading of the novel, however, though it included a careful outline of the plot, was not especially close: Trilling, despite some passages of his usual brilliance and perception, tended to summarize rather than criticize throughout much of his perhaps slightly overrated book on Forster.

Certainly Trilling's discussion of *A Passage to India* overemphasized the obviously political aspects of that novel at the expense of its underlying **metaphysical** intensity. "A Passage to India," he decided, "is the most comfortable and even the most conventional of Forster's novels. It is under the control not only of the author's insight; a huge, hulking physical fact which he is not alone in seeing, requires that the author submit to its veto-power. Consequently, this is the least surprising of Forster's novels, the least capricious and, indeed, the least personal." Though Leavis seemed to be more of an admirer of *A Passage to India* than Trilling was, calling it "a classic: not only a most significant document of our age, but a truly memorable work of literature," he saved most of his closest analyses for *Howards End*, which was the main source of disagreement. For statements about *A Passage to India* which go beyond Trilling's, therefore, we must look to more recent critics. These would include J. K. Johnstone, who in his 1954 The Bloomsbury Group carefully placed Forster in the context of that intellectual circle to which he owed so much, and James McConkey, whose 1957 *The Novels of E. M. Forster* closely analyzed Forster's writings in the so-called "New Critical" manner.

RECENT CRITICS

Even more recently, however, *A Passage to India* (along with *Howards End*) has received major attention in two brief but useful British studies and a longer, more broadly-based American one. Though all three of these critics are admirers of Trilling's book, they seem on the whole to be in somewhat greater agreement with Leavis on the relative worth of *A Passage to India* and *Howards End*. H. J. Oliver, author of a *British Book Council pamphlet on Forster* (1960), calls *A Passage to India* "to my mind" Forster's "finest novel." He disagrees with Leavis that *Howards End* is the worst of Forster's novels, however, commenting that "With all due respect to Dr. Leavis, one must prefer it to the earlier works. Lionel Trilling and others would go still further and call it 'undoubtedly Forster's masterpiece.' But, fine as *Howards End* is, Forster's masterpiece . . . is *A Passage to India*."

GRANSDEN

K. W. Gransden, whose short Evergreen Pilot series study is frequently even clearer and more perceptive than Oliver's essay, also thinks well of *Howards End*. "The book contains (Forster's) fullest and most ambitious documentation of the English social scene," he writes, "and, in the portrait of the heroine, Margaret, his most striking and completely realized character," adding that "Though Forster was still only about thirty when he wrote it, the book marks an extraordinary step towards an almost middle-aged maturity and insight into human behavior." Nevertheless, he finds some of the same flaws that Leavis does, such as "the rather contrived happy ending," and the overwritten, sentimental "Patriotic set pieces." Like Frederick Crews, an American whose book was also published in 1962, Gransden sees *A Passage to India* as Forster's masterpiece and the work of a disillusioned liberal, a liberal who had finally come to understand that the advice of *Howards End* to "Only connect" was not always a realistic possibility. "One way of looking at Forster's last novel. *A Passage to India*," he points out, "is to see it as his final corrective to liberal humanism, an ironical comment on the historically brief, egocentric Western Enlightenment. Mrs. Moore in *A Passage to India* is Mrs. Wilcox withdrawn even further from articulation, from protest, from the effort to assert in a falling world the dangerous fluency, the self-satisfaction, of Bloomsbury ethics. The entranced, static figure seated before the Marabar caves, as wooden and mum as an Indian god, de-Westernised, depersonalised, is one of the most haunting images in *A Passage to India*."

CREWS

Crews, whose full-length book is a study of Forster's intellectual background in connection with his novels, called his work E. M. Forster: *The Perils of Humanism*, and it seems almost like an expansion of Gransden's statement, quoted above-(a statement, however, which Crews may never have seen, since his book was evidently completed in 1961). On *Howards End* Crews also disagreed with Trilling, remarking that "For all its moral consistency . . . we may be permitted to wonder whether *Howards End* is, as Lionel Trilling asserts, 'undoubtedly Forster's masterpiece.' . . . the more closely we scrutinize the Wilcoxes, the less convinced we are that Forster has been able to compromise his original feelings. The outer world remains alien-panic and emptiness, telegrams and anger, the mindless destruction of personal values. Margaret's 'connection' with the Wilcoxes is merely diagrammatic . . . His plot must finally retreat to an unconvincingly 'moral' ending-it must revert to comic justice, in other words-in order to be saved from disintegration."

As for *A Passage to India*, Crews, like Oliver and Gransden, feels that it is "deservedly the best-known of Forster's novels," though he also comments that "Lionel Trilling comes closest to the truth when he says that *A Passage to India*, rather than telling us what is to be done, simply restates the familiar political and social dilemmas in the light of the total human situation." He adds, however, that "if I were to assign a single **theme** to *A Passage to India*, I would call it the incongruity between aspiration and reality. Religiously, politically, and simply in terms of the characters' efforts to get along with one another, this incongruity is pervasive. The strands of the novel are unified by the thematic principle that unity is not to be obtained, and the plot is trivial because Forster's restatements of the ordinary questions imply that all of human life, whether great or small in our customary opinion, is ensnared in pettiness."

Despite his obvious learning and the length of his careful analysis, though, Crews' discussion of *A Passage to India* is inferior to Gransden's. Indeed, of all the critics quoted here, Gransden seems most successfully to have captured, and most thoroughly to have understood, the metaphysical passion of *A Passage to India.* It "seems to say the last word," he concludes, "(not technically as Joyce seemed to) but spiritually, emotionally, morally; it drained a whole tradition to the dregs, and we are left with the alternative of contemplating an empty cup or refilling it again from the past. The novel poses infinite speculations. How far is Forster offering - and not just within the Indian framework of the story - the vague mysticism of Hinduism as a possible general corrective to the limitations of individualism, an all-inclusive salvation for a world doomed to fragmentation by its own ignorance and selfishness? How far is his final message a despairing judgment on the thrust and assertiveness of Western man since the Renaissance?" It is the posing of questions like this that makes *A Passage to India* the great work that it is. And in the last analysis, every reader must answer such questions for himself.

HOWARDS END AND A PASSAGE TO INDIA

ESSAY QUESTIONS AND ANSWERS

. . . .

Question: Why did Forster make a house the central symbol of *Howards End*?

Answer: *Howards End* is a novel about property, both spiritual and material. On the one hand, it deals with the economic structure of English society, with the complex inter-relationships of industrialists (the Wilcoxes), intellectuals (the Schlegels) and workers (the Basts) in their struggle for material property. On the other hand, it deals with the spiritual heritage, or property, of England, and the ways in which that heritage is being handled by differing groups, like the Wilcoxes, the Schlegels and the Basts. But only a house-which may also be a home-can centrally and significantly embody both the spiritual and the material aspects of property. Howards End, Ruth Wilcox's ancestral home, symbolizes both the physical roots, the landed wealth, of England, and England's spiritual heritage, the orderly ancestral tradition by which Forster believes all three English groups-the Wilcoxes, the Schlegels and the Basts-would do well to live.

Question: What are some of the other important symbols that Forster uses in *Howards End*?

Answer: A. Motorcars-which represent the rootless, restless, mechanized, modern civilization that people like the Wilcoxes are helping to build. Sealed off from the world in their motor cars, racing along at unnatural speeds, the Wilcoxes, in Forster's view, are brutally indifferent to others-as when, for instance, they kill a girl's pet cat and make no effort to console the child. It is interesting to note that Henry Wilcox's living room is upholstered in maroon leather, "as though a motor car had spawned."

B. The wych-elm-which Forster has said is a kind of genius loci, a "spirit of the place," guarding Howards End as though it were a friend or companion to the house, as though the house, with its civilized traditions, and the tree, a spirit of nature, were in a kind of partnership.

C. The Schlegel books and sword-which represent the powerful, expensive European culture that Leonard Bast aspires to but cannot attain. In the end, the intellectual meddling of the Schlegels is just as responsible for Leonard's unhappy fate as the Wilcoxes' hostile indifference, and the part the books and sword play in his death dramatizes this.

D. The child of Leonard Bast and Helen-who represents a union of lower-class aspirations and middle-class intellectual abilities to clear away the dead wood of industrial society and inherit the noblest traditions of England, embodied in *Howards End.*

Question: How did Forster use British Imperialism in *A Passage to India*?

Answer: By the end of the nineteenth century, and throughout the early twentieth century when British imperialism was in full flood, the presence of Englishmen in numerous colonies throughout the world gave many writers rich literary opportunities. Joseph Conrad, for instance, used the East in works like Youth and Victory to represent all the strangeness and glamour of the world. Rudyard Kipling, of course, used India in much the same way, and often, as in some of his short stories, he used it as Forster did, to represent the "muddle" and obstinacy of things. In *Heart of Darkness* Conrad used Africa, and the interaction of European colonists (in this case, Belgians) and Africans to make an especially profound statement about the nature of man.

Similarly, the situation of the British Raj in India gave Forster an excellent opportunity to make certain points about the difficult relations of man with his fellows, and about the incomprehensible universe in which we live. The fact that the British and the Indians are of different races, as well as more important, the fact that one nation has rather arbitrarily assumed control over the other, enabled Forster easily and realistically to outline his central ideas about human isolation and lack of connection. Furthermore, the strangeness of India-its heat, its vastness and its mysterious differentness from all that the British are used to in western civilization-made it a perfect symbol, as it often is in Kipling, for the strange and mysteriously inexplicable cosmos in which we find ourselves, a cosmos which can never be controlled or comprehended but must only be accepted with a kind of passive praise, as the Hindus in *A Passage to India* seem to be accepting it.

Question: Identify a central **theme** common to *Howards End* and *A Passage to India*

Answer: Every author has his obsessive ideas-themes and images which persist throughout the entire body of his work. Indeed, it would probably be impossible for most artists to work without such enduring preoccupations, such a philosophical background to give meaning and coherence to each individual production by setting it within a larger frame of reference. E. M. Forster is, of course, no exception to this rule. Though *Howards End* and *A Passage to India*, generally considered his two major novels, may seem to be very different in setting and story, they share a common **theme**: both are concerned with the isolation of man from man, with what Lionel Trilling has called the "separateness" that follows from either emotional insensitivity or social barriers.

In fact, though Forster deals with other themes-with problems of religion and social structure-in these two novels, "separateness" is one of his more persistent and inclusive concerns. Society is, after all, built on the relationship between man and man, and when that relationship goes wrong, society, too, goes wrong. Thus, many of the social sicknesses that Forster delineates in *Howards End* and *A Passage to India* are really rooted in the gulfs between classes and between individuals, in the failure of all to communicate and to "connect."

Religious problems, too, are often related to the **theme** of "separateness": if men cannot "connect" with each other, how can they "connect" with the universe? Mrs. Moore and Mrs. Wilcox, women somehow more mysterious and religious than the people around them, are both profoundly isolated from others. Even though Mrs. Moore becomes a kind of Hindu saint, she fails to communicate with her family and her friends; even Aziz, who worships her, is ultimately cut off from her, as, perhaps, all must inevitably be cut off from the seer, the lone individual who penetrates to the universe's "panic and emptiness" and to what is beyond it. Mrs. Wilcox too, though she is adored by her family, is absolutely misunderstood by them. She wants to leave Howards End to Margaret Schlegel, but the Wilcoxes-particularly Mr. Wilcox and Charles - are too intensely men of business, too concerned with "the outer life of telegrams and anger," to recognize her need for a "spiritual heir." Even Margaret Schlegel, who is to become that "spiritual heir," does not at first understand Mrs. Wilcox's attachment to the house, the wych-elm and the garden; at the end of the book, though she has learned much, the first Mrs. Wilcox is still somewhat shadowy to her, and, like Mrs. Moore, almost saintly.

But if both social and religious problems seem to be, in Forster's view, related to the problem of isolation, "separateness" is itself based on a kind of defect which is another of Forster's constant concerns: the problem of "the undeveloped heart . . . the undeveloped imagination," (as Lionel Trilling puts it), a problem which involves the fundamental opposition of sensitivity and insensitivity. Where positive feelings-long-term emotions of assent and identification - are no longer possible, "connection" is no longer possible. When both comprehension and communication are lost, love is lost, and each man is isolated in a universe of "panic and emptiness." Emotional harmony, which gathers together the fragments of personalities, which orders "the chaotic nature of our daily life," is only possible where there is a practical sensitivity at work, a "connection" of "the prose and the passion."

Question: Discuss the **theme** of "separateness" in *Howards End.*

Answer: In *Howards End* the most obvious separations or disconnections are social. The characters in the book can be divided into three groups: the Basts, who dwell at the extreme lower-border of the middle-class, poverty-stricken though pseudo-genteel; the Schlegels, who, as intellectuals, strive to bridge all social gulfs and thus belong to the old, classless class of scholars and artists; and the Wilcoxes, who dwell at the extreme upper border of the middle-class, wealthy, materialistic representatives of a new, commercial ruling-class, yet somehow as pseudo-genteel as the Basts are. Mrs. Wilcox, however, cannot be placed so easily. Perhaps she belongs most properly with the Schlegels as essentially classless - yet this is probably because the landed gentry, her real peers, have very nearly died out in a century of urban business. (One may say, though, that Mrs. Wilcox is, for most of the book, a kind of class unto herself, a class understood and partly identified with only by Miss Avery, the eccentric caretaker of Howards End, and to some extent by Margaret Schlegel, who becomes the second Mrs. Wilcox and in a sense a reincarnation of the first.) The simple social gulf among these three (or four) classes is a huge one.

Most obviously, the Wilcoxes are totally isolated from the Basts. Henry, warning Margaret against Leonard, says "I know the world and that type of man, and as soon as I entered the room I saw you had not been treating him properly. You must keep that type at a distance." Leonard Bast himself does not really care to associate with either the Wilcoxes or the Schlegels. To him, they are "romance," and as such they must be admired from afar. He feels that his separation from them is complete and that the possibility of "connection" with them is remote. Yet the Basts are, in many ways, similar to the Wilcoxes. Both groups are, for instance, profoundly suspicious. Leonard thinks that Helen may have taken his umbrella on purpose; when Margaret reminds Henry of his affair with Mrs. Bast, he cries "I perceive you are attempting blackmail." And it is significant that both groups are really more suspicious of the Schlegels than they are of each other.

The Wilcoxes and the Basts accept the world as it is, accept a "nomadic," fragmented existence of isolation and uncertainty. The Schlegels refuse to. Helen, perhaps over-intense, over-theoretical, tries to "connect" with the Basts. Margaret, more level-headed but, in some ways, equally theoretical, tries to "connect" with the Wilcoxes. Neither succeeds absolutely, though neither quite fails. The Basts and the Wilcoxes are dense, insensitive; yet each group has in it a spark which can respond to the Schlegel's sensitivity. Leonard is "adventurous," Henry is "practical," and the spirits of adventure and practicality are fused, by Helen and Margaret, at the close of the book, into a new and transcendent spirit of comprehension and "connection," much like the first Mrs. Wilcox's.

Even within each class, however, communication fails, and each character is, for the most part, isolated. Mrs. Wilcox certainly cannot make herself understood. "She and daily life" are "out of focus," and though she is loved, she is rarely known. Aunt Juley entirely misunderstands the Schlegels. Tibby is stony, snobbish, indifferent to the problems of others. Helen is perpetually trying to bridge gulfs but generally fails, except with her sister, because she usually acts from the brain rather than from the heart. The Wilcoxes are familiar with each other, but since there is little to know about each, know nothing. They shrink from emotion and romp athletically away from all forms of social sensitivity. Henry, though slightly superior to his children, has built a "fortress" of business around himself and can never quite "get through." Margaret alone knows that "he desired comradeship and affection, but he feared them . . ." And Margaret herself, though she does often bridge gulfs successfully, and though she is primarily responsible for the temporary "connection" established in the last chapter of the book, is ultimately isolated. "If he (Henry) was a fortress,"

Forster says, "she was a mountain peak, whom all might tread, but whom the snows made nightly virginal."

Despite her own isolation, however, it is through Margaret that a kind of union is finally achieved. Helen and her child by Leonard Bast, Henry Wilcox and Margaret herself, who has become his wife, retreat to Howards End and cling there, brooded over by the sensitive, comprehensive spirit of Mrs. Wilcox, the spirit of the earth which draws all together. They know that London is encroaching, that sooner or later a disjointed "nomadic" civilization will overwhelm this stable, landed unity, this life of "significant soil," but at least for the time being some distances have been diminished.

Question: Discuss the **theme** of "separateness" in *A Passage to India*, and summarize it with reference to both novels.

Answer: In *A Passage to India*, Lionel Trilling remarks, "the **theme** of separateness, of fences and barriers . . . is . . . everywhere dominant. The separation of race from race, sex from sex, culture from culture, even of man from himself, is what underlies every relationship." And, indeed, while *Howards End* is in some ways an easier book, *A Passage to India* is in many respects more striking. The gulfs between men are mercilessly revealed throughout, and what seems to be an enormous though temporary pessimism descends at the end; the universe, at this point, assents to separation, to the division of Fielding and Aziz and perhaps to the division of all men.

As in *Howards End* the most obvious gulfs in *A Passage to India* are social and, because of the book's setting, racial. All Englishmen separate themselves from all Indians. Dr. Panna Lal, among others, tries to ingratiate himself with his white rulers, but his courtesy becomes servility. More importantly, Fielding remarks that the "white" men are not really white but "pinko-grey" and aligns himself with the Indians at the trial of Aziz-yet even he, when on leave from India he first catches sight of Venice, is refreshed by western order and western style. The Indians themselves are separated from each other. Moslems do not quite respect Hindus; Hindus do not quite respect Moslems; Jains, Sikhs, others sects, all are isolated, unable to communicate.

Within the English group, too, there are important gulfs. Fielding is something of an outcast, a traitor to British imperialism. Mrs. Moore, who becomes a Hindu saint, must be bundled out of the country by her dull, worried son. Adela Quested is pronounced "not pukka" because, in her own ineffectual blue-stocking way, she is seeking for "the real India." At the "Bridge-Party" these social and racial gulfs are given their "objective correlative": on one side of the lawn stand the English ladies and their menfolk, querulous, distressed at the presence of so many Indians; on the other side of the lawn stand the Indians, embarrassed, some servile, some faintly contemptuous, regarding the disgruntled English with a kind of nervous curiosity. Mrs. Moore and Adela flicker between the two groups-Adela, who is to "betray" both, Mrs. Moore who will not formally affiliate with either but who will become the saint of one - and Fielding "romps" among the Indians, still very British somehow, but trying, trying, to become the "Bridge" that the "Party" lacks.

On a more personal and perhaps more profound level, everyone in *A Passage to India* is isolated throughout. "Our loneliness . . . our isolation, our need for the Friend who never comes . . ." is omnipresent, yet there is not a single character in the book who seems capable of acting on this need. Adela and Ronny, though they plan to marry, are not really in love and have never really understood each other. Mrs. Moore, reflecting on this, thinks that "the human race would have become a single person centuries ago if marriage was any use." When connection is attempted, as between Adela and Fielding after the trial, "a friendliness, as of dwarfs shaking hands" is "in the air." Later, when Fielding is passionately in love with his wife, Stella, he fears that she does not return his feelings.

Even the callous English women seek, at times, the "tender core of the heart that is so seldom used . . ." and yet they cannot, of course really find it or use it. Helen, in *Howards End*, had believed that "personal relations are the important thing for ever and ever . . ." And Adela, like Fielding and Aziz and several others in *A Passage to India*, echoes this belief, but asks pessimistically "What is the use of personal relationships when everyone brings less and less to them?" Ronny and the other efficient white rulers of India are men with "business minds," just as Charles and Henry Wilcox were; they are practical and insensitive, and "where there is officialism every human relationship suffers." Still, these relationships are of paramount importance. Fielding, at one point, recognizes their significance and "fatigued by the merciless and enormous day," loses "his usual sane view of human intercourse" and feels "that we exist not in ourselves but in terms of each other's minds."

Even - and perhaps especially - Mrs. Moore, who dominates the book, just as, to a lesser extent, Mrs. Wilcox and Margaret dominate *Howards End*, even she fails absolutely to communicate. Though, like Mrs. Wilcox, she is loved, even worshipped, she cannot escape herself and her own despairing vision, in the Marabar caves, of infinite, universal nothingness, coupled with the sort of human "panic and emptiness" that haunted Helen Schlegel throughout *Howards End*. In the caves she realizes that she doesn't "want to write to anyone," and doesn't "want to communicate with anyone, not even with God." Any attempt at a relationship of any kind is futile - and "I'll retire into a cave of my own," she says, renouncing the world of God, the world of man, and affirming that the only reality in the universe is the world of the self, forever single and obscure.

Despite Mrs. Moore's decision, the world of the self is shown throughout *Howards End* and *A Passage to India* as, like the world of all men, often fragmented, separated from within, chopped into a number of clamorous, discordant bits and pieces. And insensitivity is rooted precisely in such divisions of personality. Without inner wholeness, without inner coherence, there can be no outer wholeness or coherence; "connection," the external bridge, is built upon an internal bridge, the emotional unity that comes from self-knowledge, from such years of devotion to "the inner life" as Margaret and Helen Schlegel have spent. Margaret, who, of all the characters in both books, comes closest to successfully maintaining inner and outer "connections," hopes that "she might be able to help (Henry) to the building of the rainbow bridge that should connect the prose in us with the passion. Without it we are meaningless fragments, half monks, half beasts, unconnected arches that have never joined into a man. With it, love is born, and alights on the highest curve . . ." For Henry is a new type of man, a type of whom Forster says that "perhaps the little thing that says 'I' is missing out of the middle of their heads." And lacking that instrument, lacking the supreme and sane ego which is capable of "connection" and of love, man is, as Mrs. Moore reflects at one point, "no nearer to understanding man" than he has ever been.

The opposition between coherence and "separateness," then, involving oppositions between social, personal and religious wholeness and fragmentation, is a major problem that concerns Forster throughout both *Howards End* and *A Passage to India*. He seems to feel, however, that man's isolation from man, from God, and from himself, though tragic and perhaps inevitable, can, nonetheless, be transcended at the proper times. The parting of Aziz and Fielding, though apparently sanctioned by all of nature, may not be final. In a universe where "panic and emptiness" are so possible, in a civilization where the vistas of "panic and emptiness" are constantly being enlarged, Forster admonishes men not only to "connect" the "prose and the passion" in themselves, but, on the basis of such fusion, to "connect" with each other. The personal, even where, as in India, it is not always possible, is supremely valuable. Mrs. Moore's retreat from society and vision of the universe is not the final salvation accessible to man. Forster seems to believe that the fusion of man with man, class with class, in marriage and parenthood, which is hinted at in the conclusion of *Howards End* and in the festival of love at the close of *A Passage to India*, may be the product of a greater struggle, the reflection of a greater glory.

BIBLIOGRAPHY

· ·

THE NOVELS OF E. M. FORSTER (GENERAL)

Suggested topics for papers: How do *Howards End* and *A Passage to India* relate to Forster's earlier novels? To each other? What developments do they indicate in his style? In his philosophy? What general judgments have been made about Forster's position among contemporary novelists?

Burra, Peter. "The Novels of E. M. Forster," in *The Nineteenth Century and After*, CXVI (1934), pp. 581-594; reprinted as an introduction to the Everyman edition of *A Passage to India* (London, 1942).

Furbank, P. N., and F. J. H. Haskell. Interview with E. M. Forster in *The Paris Review*, Spring 1953. Reprinted in *Writers at Work*, ed. Malcolm Cowley (London, 1958), pp. 23-33.

Gerber, Helmut E. *A Check List of Writings on E. M. Forster*, published in *English Fiction* in *Transition 1880-1920* (Purdue University, Indiana, 1959). This is an extremely useful listing of all the available critical material on Forster, which contains over one hundred items. Serious students of *Howards End* and *A Passage to India* are referred to Gerber's *Check List* as a supplement to this Bibliography.

Gransden, K. W. *E. M. Forster* (New York, 1962). A brief and useful critical introduction to Forster in the Evergreen Pilot series on contemporary writers. Contains a chapter on each of the major novels, as well as sections on the short stories and the criticism.

Leavis, F. R. "E. M. Forster," in *Scrutiny*, VII (1938), pp. 185-202. Reprinted in *The Common Pursuit* (London, 1952) and in *The Importance of Scrutiny* (New York, 1948). A discussion of Forster's place on the literary scene by one of England's leading and most controversial literary critics.

Macauley, Rose. *The Writings of E. M. Forster* (London, 1938). Analysis of Forster by a fellow English novelist.

McConkey, James. *The Novels of E. M. Forster* (Ithaca, 1957). Close "New Critical" examinations of all five novels.

Oliver, H. J. *The Art of E. M. Forster* (London, 1960). A short discussion of Forster's major works, with special emphasis placed on *Howards End* and *A Passage to India.*

Trilling, Lionel. *E. M. Forster* (New York, 1944). A brief, in many respects brilliant treatment of Forster's works, novel by novel, by one of America's leading literary critics. Though it is not as thorough as it might be, this is probably the best known and the most highly regarded book about Forster to be written so far.

Warner, Rex. E. M. Forster, *Writers and their Work* (London, 1950).

Wilson, Angus. "A Conversation with E. M. Forster," *In Encounter* IX, (1957), pp. 52-57.

HOWARDS END (IN ADDITION TO THE CHAPTERS IN WORKS LISTED ABOVE).

Suggested topics for papers: *Howards End* and English tradition. The patriotism of *Howards End*. *Howards End* and England's future. *Howards End* and the Industrial Revolution. The economics of *Howards End*. Forster and Samuel Butler: A comparison of *Howards End* and *The Way of All Flesh*. Forster and Shaw: Margaret Schlegel's theories compared to Andrew Undershaft's (in *Major Barbara*). The symbolism of *Howards End*. The supernatural in *Howards End*.

Bradbury, Malcolm. "E. M. Forster's *Howards End*." *Critical Quarterly* IV (1962), 229-214.

Churchill, Thomas. "Place and Personality in *Howards End*." *Critique* V (1962), 61-73.

Hoffman, Frederick J. "*Howards End* and the Bogey of Progress." *Modern Fiction Studies* (1961), VII, 258-270.

Hoy, Cyrus. "Forster's **Metaphysical** Novel." *PMLA*, LXXV (1960), 126-136.

Shahane, V. A. "Beethoven's Fifth Symphony in *Howards End*." *Indian Journal of English Studies*, I (1960), 100-103.

Thomson, George H. "**Theme** and Symbol in *Howards End*." *Modern Fiction Studies*, VII, (1961), 229-242.

A PASSAGE TO INDIA (IN ADDITION TO CHAPTERS OF WORKS LISTED IN SECTION ONE).

Suggested topics for papers: Forster and India. Forster and the British Raj in India. *The Hill of Devi* and *A Passage to India*. Walt Whitman's "Passage to

India" and Forster's *A Passage to India*. Forster's view of India in *A Passage to India* compared to Rudyard Kipling's in Kim or Plain Tales From the Hills. Rudyard Kipling's "The Bridge-Builders" and *A Passage to India*. The metaphysics of *A Passage to India*. Hinduism and *A Passage to India*. The symbolism of the caves in *A Passage to India*. The supernatural in *A Passage to India*. **Foreshadowings** of Existentialism in *A Passage to India*. The pessimism of *A Passage to India*. Indian nationalism and *A Passage to India*. Mrs. Moore and Mrs. Wilcox: two strong women. Harcourt, Brace & World, Inc., is the publisher for the above mentioned *The Hill of Devi* and *The Death of the Moth*. Brander, Laurence. "E. M. Forster and India." *Review of English Literature* (Leeds) III (1962), iv, 76-84.

Clubb, Roger L. "*A Passage to India*: The Meaning of the Marabar Caves." *College Language Association Journal*, VI (1963), 194-198.

Dauner, Louise. "What Happened in the Cave? Reflections on *A Passage to India*." *Modern Fiction Studies*, VII (1961), 258-270.

Forster, E. M. *The Hill of Devi*. New York, 1953.

Hale, Nancy. "A Passage to Relationship." *Antioch Review*, XX (1960), 19-30.

Hollingsworth, Keith. "*A Passage to India*: The Echoes in the Marabar Caves." *Criticism*, IV (1962), 210-224.

Kain, Richard M. "Vision and Discovery in E. M. Forster's *A Passage to India*." *Twelve Original Essays* (24), pp. 253-275.

Shusterman, David. "The Curious Case of Professor Godbole: *A Passage to India* Re-Examined." PMLA, LXXVI (1961), 426-435.

Thomson, George H. "Thematic Symbol in *A Passage to India*," *Twentieth Century Literature*, VII (1961), 51-63.

FORSTER AND BLOOMSBURY: FORSTER'S INTELLECTUAL BACKGROUND.

Suggested topics: *The changing philosophy of E. M. Forster.* Forster's relationship within the Bloomsbury Group. Forster and Virginia Woolf. Forster's influence on Bloomsbury. G. E. Moore's influence on Forster. Forster and Goldsworthy Lowes Dickinson. Forster's liberalism. Forster's humanism. Auto-biographical elements in *Howards End* and *A Passage to India.*

Crews, Frederick C. *E. M. Forster: The Perils of Humanism.* (Princeton, 1962). A thorough and well-grounded discussion of Forster's five novels-especially emphasizing *Howards End* and *A Passage to India*-in connection with the author's intellectual background, his "philosophical liberalism" and "skeptical humanism." Should be very valuable to serious students of Forster.

Hannah, Donald. "The Limitations of Liberalism in E. M. Forster's Work." *English Miscellany*, XIII (1962), 165-178.

Johnstone, J. K. *The Bloomsbury Group* (The New York, 1954). An excellent history of the Bloomsbury intellectuals and their place in contemporary literary history. Johnstone pays special attention to the works of Forster, Lytton Strachey and Virginia Woolf, and the section of Forster contains good analyses of all five novels.

Leavis, F. R. "E. M. Forster." (See Section I). Criticism by a well-known opponent of Bloomsbury.

Macdonald, Alastair A. "Class-Consciousness in E. M. Forster." *University of Kansas City Review*, XXVII (1961), 235-240.

Woolf, Virginia. "The Novels of E. M. Forster," in *The Death of the Moth* (London, 1942). An appreciation by one of the most famous members of the Bloomsbury Group.

CPSIA information can be obtained
at www.ICGtesting.com
Printed in the USA
LVHW020517020720
659501LV00017B/620